Charles Newhall Taintor, Charles Newhall] [from old catalog] [Taintor

The Hudson River from New York to Albany

Charles Newhall Taintor, Charles Newhall] (from old catalog) [Taintor

The Hudson River from New York to Albany

ISBN/EAN: 9783337374587

Printed in Europe, USA, Canada, Australia, Japan

Cover: Foto ©Andreas Hilbeck / pixelio.de

More available books at **www.hansebooks.com**

Taintor's Route and City Guides

THE HUDSON RIVER
AS SEEN BY
Passengers on the River Steamers.

TAINTOR BROTHERS & CO.
758 Broadway, New York.

RIGAUD & CO.'S PERFUMERY.

RIGAUD'S NEW PERFUMES
FOR THE HANDKERCHIEF

Are recommended as unsurpassed by any similar articles, both for delicacy of perfume and permanence. The following are especially recommended:

Extracts of YLANG YLANG,
CHAMPACA,
KANANGA,
ALSO ALL THE STANDARD PERFUMES OF THE DAY.

Special attention is called also to Rigaud's Exquisite Toilet Preparations; Dentifrices; Preparations for the Complexion; Pomades, Oils, and Washes for the Hair; Fine Toilet Soaps, which are offered in great variety. Send for Rigaud & Co.'s Toilet Guide, which is mailed free by

E. FOUGERA & CO., Agents for the United States,
30 North William St., New York.

DELACRE'S CHOCOLATES.

The attention of Connoisseurs in Chocolate is directed to the above Chocolates, which for purity and fine aroma are
UNSURPASSED.
WE NOW OFFER THE FOLLOWING QUALITIES:
SANTÉ FIN; SANTÉ SURFIN; VANILLA FIN; VANILLA SURFIN; also HOMŒOPATHIC CHOCOLATE, and DELACRE'S EXTRACT OF MEAT CHOCOLATE,

An excellent Tonic for Invalids and Convalescents.

Consumers unable to obtain this brand will please send their orders or inquiries to

E. FOUGERA & Co., Agents,
30 NORTH WILLIAM ST., NEW YORK.

THE TRAVELERS

OLDEST IN AMERICA.   LARGEST IN THE WORLD.

LIFE AND ACCIDENT NSURANCE COMPANY,
HARTFORD, CONN.

SH ASSETS over $3,750,000
RPLUS TO POLICY HOLDERS, ... 1,500,000
ID IN CASH BENEFITS over , . . . 3,000,000

Accident Policies Written, over . . 400,000
Accident Claims Paid, over . . . 24,000

ae in seventeen of the whole number insured have thus ived the practical benefits of Accident Insurance.

General Accident Policies, for year or month, written by Agents without delay. No medical examination required. Yearly cost, $5 to $10 per $1,000 for occupations not specially hazardous.

LIFE AND ENDOWMENT INSURANCE.
All approved forms at Low Cash Prices.

JAMES G. BATTERSON, President.
RODNEY DENNIS, Sec'y.   JOHN E. MORRIS, Ass't Sec'y.
NEW YORK OFFICE, 207 BROADWAY.
Agents everywhere in United States and Canadas.

PERRY & COMPANY,

MANUFACTURERS OF THE

ARGAND BASE BURNER
THE BELMONT RANGE,
THE CUNARD COOK,

And one hundred and twenty-five other patterns of

STOVES, RANGES, AND HOT-AIR FURNACES.

NEW YORK CITY,	ALBANY,	CHICAGO,
86 Beekman St.	115 Hudson Ave.	15 and 17 Lake St.

C. H. COVELL,

922 Broadway, N. E. Corner 21st Street,

IMPORTER OF AND DEALER IN

Clocks, Bronzes,
AND
FANCY GOODS,

CHANDELIERS AND GAS FIXTURES,

ALSO, FIXTURES FOR OIL LAMPS,
Of most approved patterns.

CONSTANTLY RECEIVING PER STEAMER

Novelties at Popular Prices.

LADIES! ASK FOR

(Wound on White Spools.)
GEORGE A. CLARK,   Sole Agent.
And MILWARD'S HELIX NEEDLES in patent wrappers,
They are the best in use.   Sold Everywhere.

Phelps, Dodge & Co.,

CLIFF ST., between John and Fulton,
New York.

IMPORTERS AND DEALERS IN

TIN AND ROOFING PLATES,
OF ALL SIZES AND KINDS,

PIG TIN, RUSSIA SHEET IRON,
Charcoal and Common Sheet Iron,

LEAD, SHEET ZINC, COPPER,
SPELTER, SOLDER, ANTIMONY, &c.

MANUFACTURERS OF

COPPER, BRASS, AND WIRE.

An indispensable requisite *for every Teacher, Advanced Student, Intelligent Family, Library, and Professional Person, is*
THE BEST ENGLISH DICTIONARY.

WEBSTER'S UNABRIDGED.
10,000 *Words and Meanings not in other Dictionaries.*
3,000 Engravings; 1,840 Pages Quarto. Price, $12.
FOUR PAGES COLORED ILLUSTRATIONS.

"THE BEST PRACTICAL ENGLISH DICTIONARY EXTANT."—
London Quarterly Review, Oct., 1873.

The sales of Webster's Dictionaries throughout the country in 1873 were 20 times as large as the sales of any other Dictionaries.

One family of children having WEBSTER'S UNABRIDGED, and using it freely, and another not having it, the first will become much the most intelligent men and women. Ask your teacher or minister if it is not so, then buy the book and use, and urge its use, freely.

Published by
G. & C. MERRIAM, Springfield, Mass.

SPRINGFIELD
Fire and Marine Insurance Co.

INCORPORATED 1849.   CHARTER PERPETUAL.
NO MARINE RISKS TAKEN.

Capital, - - - - - - $750,000.00
Cash Assets, - - - - - 1,500,000.00

DWIGHT R. SMITH, Pres't.
S. J. HALL, Sec'y.   A. J. WRIGHT, Treas.

BIGELOW, COIT & PECK, Agents, - - - - NEW YORK.
ALEX. W. WISTER, Agent, - - - - - PHILADELPHIA.
REED & BROTHER, Agents, - - - - - BOSTON.

Agencies also in all the principal Cities and Towns in the country.

A. J. HARDING, Gen'l Agt.
Western Department,   Chicago, Ill.

MOSELEY'S NEW HAVEN HOUSE,
FRONTING THE PARK AND OPPOSITE YALE COLLEGE.

Is owned and kept by S. H. MOSELEY, who for ten years was connected with the famous Massasoit House, Springfield, Mass., and for five years partner of the charming Brevoort House, New York. It is the most complete, comfortable and homelike Hotel in the City, and one of the best to be found in this country. Mr. Moseley also has the Restaurant at the Railway Station, which is the best eating place for passengers between New York and Boston. All express trains stop ten minutes at New Haven.

BREVOORT HOUSE,
NEW YORK.

This well known Hotel is located on

FIFTH AVENUE, cor. of EIGHTH STREET,

Near Washington Square.

One of the most delightful situations, combining the quiet retirement of a private mansion with easy access to all parts of the city.

The Brevoort has always been a

FAVORITE WITH EUROPEANS

visiting the United States, the plan upon which it is kept being such as to commend it to those accustomed to European habits.

CHARLES C. WAITE,
Resident Proprietor.

WINDSOR HOTEL,

FIFTH AVENUE, 46th & 47th STS., NEW YORK.

HAWK, WAITE, & WETHERBEE, Proprietors.

The Windsor is more magnificent and commodious, and contains more real comforts, than any other Hotel in America.

Its location is delightful, being surrounded by the most fashionable residences in New York; it is also near the famous Central Park and within three minutes' walk of the Grand Central Railway Station. The rooms, with all the modern improvements, are especially adapted for travelers; this Hotel also has elegant apartments, *en suite* for families, permanent or transient. The light, ventilation, and sanitary qualities are perfect, and cannot be excelled.

SAMUEL HAWK,   CHAS. C. WAITE,   GARDNER WETHERBEE,
of St. Nicholas Hotel,   of Brevoort House,   late of Revere House, Boston.

CONNECTICUT MUTUAL LIFE INSURANCE CO.,
OF HARTFORD, CONN.
Thirtieth Annual Statement.

Net Assets, January 1, 1875		$38,826,267 12
Received in 1875: For Premiums	$7,365,468 53	
For Interest and Rents	2,654,931 81	9,835,400 34
		48,626,683 21
Disbursed in 1875		7,164,032 68
Balance, Net Assets, December 31, 1875		$41,462,665 53
Gross assets, December 31, 1875		$43,494,656 92
Liabilities:		
Amount required to reinsure all outstanding policies, net, assuming 4 per cent. interest	$35,494,015 00	
Extra Reserve	197,612 00	
All other liabilities	798,142 00	39,489,799 00
Surplus, December 31, 1875		$ 4,004,851 92
Increase of assets during 1875		$3,050,954 96
Ratio of expense of management to receipts in 1875		7.65 per cent.
Policies in force, Dec. 31, 1875, 66,249, insuring		$155,078,842 00

JAMES GOODWIN, President.
JACOB L. GREENE, Sec. **JOHN M. TAYLOR**, Asst. Sec.

Secure your Valuables by Depositing in Fire and Burglar Proof Vaults, Thoroughly Ventilated and Positively Free from Dampness.

CENTRAL SAFE DEPOSIT CO.
71 & 73 West 23d Street, Masonic Temple Building.

Silver received on deposit for the season at low rates. Packages will be sent for and delivered FREE OF CHARGE. VALUABLE PAINTINGS STORED FOR ANY LENGTH OF TIME IN A ROOM SPECIALLY FOR THE PURPOSE.

Trunks of clothing received on deposit (accessible at all times to the owner), 50 cents per month. Small Safes to rent by the year or month in Fire and Burglar Proof Vault at from $10 to $100 per year. An examination of the premises is requested before depositing elsewhere.

DIRECTORS.
Chas. Roome, Pres. Manhattan Gas Co.; Darius R. Mangan, Pres. National Trust Co.; Edward V. Loew, Pres. Manuf. & Builders' Fire Ins.Co.; Geo. Pancoast, Pres. Archer & Pancoast Manuf. Co.; Edward B. Bulkley, Pres. Jefferson Iron Co.; Alex. M. Lesley, Pres. Trades Savings Bank.; Thos. L. James, Postmaster. New York.; Geo. E. Sterry, Weaver & Sterry, Importers of Drugs.; Wm. H. Howell, Howell, Barr & Co., Dealers in Syrups.; Archibald Hance, Sup't Dry Dock, E. B. & R. R. R. Co.; Ellwood E. Thorne, 71 & 73 West 23d Street.

ELLWOOD E. THORNE, *President.*
JOHN P. ROBERTS, Sec'y & Treas. WILLIAM A. FRAZER, Supt.

THE
HUDSON RIVER

FROM

NEW YORK TO ALBANY,

AS SEEN FROM THE

"DAY LINE" AND OTHER STEAMERS,

WITH

DESCRIPTIVE SKETCHES OF CITIES, VILLAGES, STATIONS,
SCENERY, AND OBJECTS OF INTEREST ALONG
THE ROUTE.

ILLUSTRATED WITH MAPS AND WOODCUTS.

Copyright, Taintor Brothers & Co., 1875.

NEW YORK:
TAINTOR BROTHERS & CO.,
758 Broadway.

LE BOUTILLIER BROTHERS,

48 EAST 14th STREET, NEW YORK,

IMPORTERS AND RETAILERS OF

BLACK AND COLORED SILKS,
DRESS GOODS OF EVERY DESCRIPTION,
MOURNING GOODS OF ALL KINDS,
LINENS AND WHITE GOODS,
HOSIERY,
UNDERVESTS AND DRAWERS,
PARIS AND DOMESTIC UNDERGARMENTS,
EMBROIDERIES,
LACES,
HANDKERCHIEFS,
RIBBONS, NECK-WEAR, Etc.

PERINOT KID GLOVES.

We call especial attention to our Stock, comprising all the new and desirable styles, which we offer at the VERY LOWEST prices.

Samples sent free on application.

LE BOUTILLIER BROTHERS,

48 East 14th Street,	NEW YORK.
912 Chestnut Street,	PHILADELPHIA.
104 and 106 West 4th St.,	CINCINNATI.
2 Faubourg Poissonnier,	PARIS.

INDEX.

Albany,	53
André and Arnold,	22
Athens,	50
Barnegat,	36
Barrytown,	39
Capture of Stony Point,	28
Carmansville,	15
Castleton, N. Y.	51
Catskill,	41
Catskill Mountains,	42
Coeyman's	51
Cold Spring,	32
Columbiaville,	50
Cornwall Landing,	33
Coxsackie,	50
Croton Point,	25
Day Line Steamers,	12
Dobbs' Ferry,	19
Fishkill Landing,	34
Fort Clinton,	30
Fort Lee,	16
Fort Montgomery,	30
Fort Washington,	13
Germantown,	40
Greenbush,	52
Hastings,	18
Haverstraw,	26
Hoboken,	14
Hudson,	50
HUDSON RIVER,	5
Hyde Park,	37
Irvington,	20
Jersey City,	14
Kingston,	38
Low Point,	35
Manhattanville,	15
Marlborough,	35
Milton Ferry,	36
New Baltimore,	51
Newburgh,	34
New Hamburgh,	35
New Paltz,	37
Nyack,	25
Peekskill,	29
Piermont,	19
Poughkeepsie,	36
Rhinebeck,	39
Riverdale,	17
Rondout,	38
Saugerties,	40
Schodac,	51
Sing Sing,	25
Spuyten Duyvil,	16
Staatsburg,	37
Stony Point,	26
Stuyvesant,	51
Tarrytown,	20
Teller's Point,	25
Tivoli,	40
Verplanck's Point,	26
Weehawken,	14
West Point,	31
Yonkers,	18

GRAND UNION HOTEL,
Opposite Grand Central Depot, New York.
Baggage taken to and from this Depot to Hotel free. European plan Restaurant supplied with the best. Prices moderate.
W. D. GARRISON.

THE
DSON

York
nor"s
o,
bank
nk in

cinity
is the
itable

two

with
Post

Store,

, and

ple.
t, and

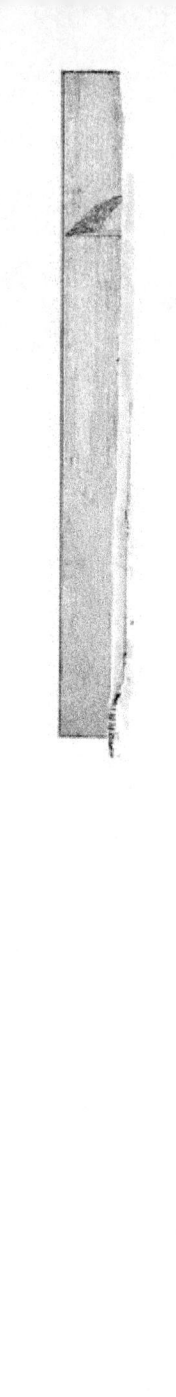

PANORAMA OF THE HUDSON.

PROMINENT OBJECTS OF INTEREST THAT MAY BE SEEN FROM THE STEAMERS OF THE "DAY LINE," ON THE TRIP OF THE HUDSON FROM NEW YORK TO ALBANY.

As the steamer puts out from the dock, a fine view of *New York Harbor* is disclosed to the south, with *Castle Williamson* and *Governor's Island, Brooklyn, The Narrows*, and *Staten Island* in the distance.

In the following arrangement the points of interest on the west bank of the river are placed in the left hand, and those on the east bank in the right-hand column.

WEST BANK.

Jersey City, pop. 100,000; terminus of Pennsylvania R. R., Central N. J., Midland, Erie, and Northern N. J. Railroads. Cunard Steamers' docks. Opposite dock of Day Line is Erie Depot.

Bergen Heights in distance.

Hoboken, a little north, pop. 30,000; terminus of Delaware and Lackawanna R. R. and Hamburg Line of Steamers.

Stevens Institute and *Stevens Mansion*, on *Castle Hill*, in northern part of Hoboken.

Elysian Fields, just north.

EAST BANK.

New York City, with *Trinity* and *St. Paul's Spires* towards the south, *St. John's Spire* west.

Prominent Buildings: *Equitable Life Insurance*, near Trinity. *Western Union Telegraph*. *U. S. Post Office*, with two domes, and *City Hall* north. *N. Y. Tribune* building, with sharp tower, just east of Post Office.

Grand Central Hotel.

Further north is *Stewart's Store*, cor. Broadway and 10th St.

Masonic Temple, 6th Ave. and 23d St.

Booth's Theater, opp. Temple.

Manhattan Market, 34th St. and 10th Ave.

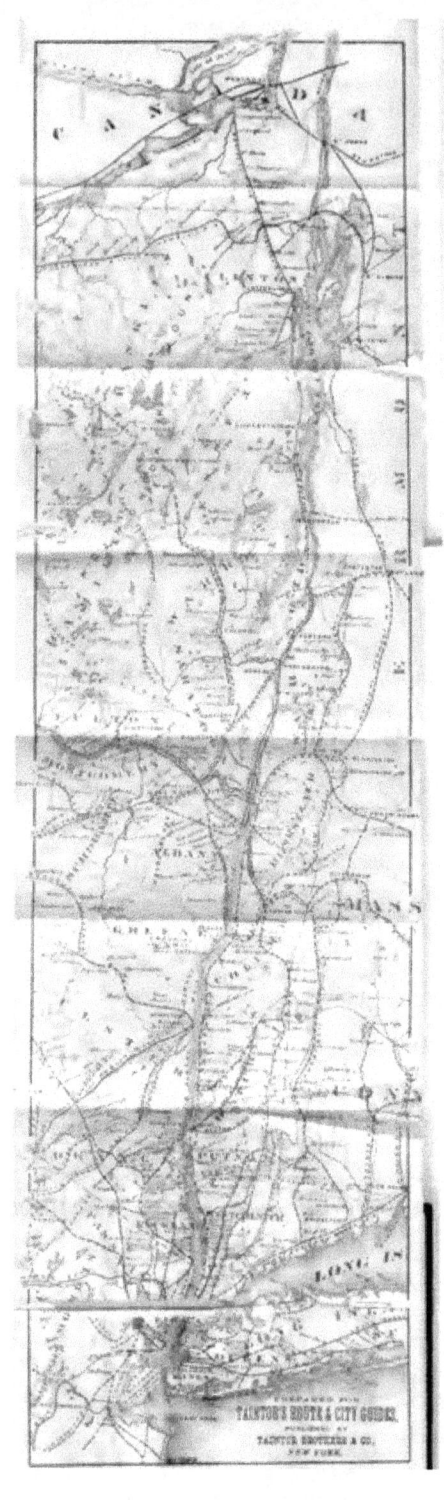

HUDSON RIVER.   111

WEST BANK.

Weehawken, scene of Hamilton and Burr duel.

Seven-story White Building above Weehawken is a brewery.

Tillie Tendlem, opposite Carmansville.

Fort Lee, ten miles from New York, opposite Deaf and Dumb Asylum. The site of the old fort is marked by a flagstaff on the bluff.

The Palisades begin at Fort Lee and extend 15 miles to the north, from 200 to 500 feet in height.

Palisade Mountain Hotel, opposite Inwood.

The Palisades stretch along, an unbroken wall of columnar traprock, for nearly 20 miles, varying in height from 200 to 500 feet above the river.

Indian Head, the highest point of the Palisades, 550 feet above the river.

Tappan Bay, or *Tappan Zee*, extending north 15 miles to Croton Point, nearly four miles wide.

EAST BANK.

St. Thomas Church Spire, 5th Ave. and 53d St.
Sixty-Fifth St., New York, N. Y. Orphan Asylum.
Jones Hill—shooting gallery near the river.
Bloomingdale Lunatic Asylum, bet. 115th and 120th Sts.
Manhattanville, 132d St.
Iron Works, with
Carmansville, home of Audubon, naturalist, just above.
Old Claremont Hotel, near river.
Trinity Cemetery—above hotel.
N. Y. Institute for Deaf &-Dumb.
Jeffrey's Hook, a point jutting into the river—site of old fort.
Washington Heights, 185th St.
Fort Washington, 10 miles from New York. Site near James Gordon Bennett's residence, with gilded dome.
Inwood, once known as Tubby Hook.
Spuyten Duyvil Creek, or Harlem River. Main line of Hudson River R. R. diverges from river through cut to Grand Central Depot, 42d St., New York.
Westchester Heights.
Riverdale, 14 miles from N. Y.
Convent and Academy of Mount St. Vincent, with
Font Hill in front, built by Edwin Forrest.
Yonkers, 17 miles from New York. Pop. 20,000. Site of old Phillipse Mansion.

HUDSON RIVER.

WEST BANK.

Piermont, twenty-four miles from New York; formerly terminus of Erie Railway. Pier one mile long, extending into river. Palisade formation terminates here. Boundary between New York and New Jersey.

Nyack, with *Rockland Female Institute* near river, and *Ramapo Mountains* in distance, 600 feet high.

Upper Nyack, one mile above Nyack.

Rockland Lake, among the hills, opposite Sing Sing. Source of Hackensack river, and great ice-quarry in winter.

Ramapo Mountain.

Haverstraw Bay, five miles wide—the widest part of the Hudson, extending from Croton Point on the south to Verplanck's Point on the north.

High Thorn Mountain—a sharp peak near Haverstraw.

Haverstraw Village—with two miles of brick-yards.

Treason Hill, north of Haverstraw, where Arnold met André at Joshua Hett Smith's.

Grassy Point, two miles north of Haverstraw.

Stony Point, one mile north of Grassy Point.

Tompkins Cove—with limekilns and quarry.

Kidd's Point, now Caldwell's.

EAST BANK.

Spring Hill Grove.

Dudley's Grove above.

Hastings-on-the-Hudson, 21 miles from New York. Sugar Refinery near river.

Dobbs' Ferry, 22 miles fr. N. Y.

Irvington, 24 miles from N. Y.

Sunnyside, home of Washington Irving, ½ mile north of R. R. Station, scarcely visible through the trees, near the river.

Tarrytown, 29 miles from New York. Pop. 5,000. Steamer stops beside ferryboat in middle of the river, transferring passengers for both Tarrytown and Nyack.

Sing Sing, 32 miles from New York. Pop. 3,000.

State Prison, near the river, south of the village, built of white marble.

Croton River empties into Hudson 1 mile north of Sing Sing.

Croton Point, just above Croton River—junction of Tappan Bay and Haverstraw Bay. Extreme projection is called

Teller's Point. Off this point the Vulture anchored when she brought André to meet Arnold.

Croton Village above.

Montrosse's Point.

Verplanck's Point.

King's Ferry before Revolution—between these two points ½ mile.

HUDSON RIVER.

WEST BANK.	EAST BANK.
Donderberg Mt., 1,000 ft high.	*Peekskill.* Pop. 6,000. 43 miles from New York.
Iona Island—with grapery and famous pic-nic grounds.	*Nameless Highland.*
Fort Montgomery Creek, opposite Anthony's Nose.	*The Race*, between Iona Island and east bank of river.
Fort Clinton south side creek.	*Anthony's Nose*, 1,200 feet high with R. R. Tunnel near river.
Fort Montgomery on north side.	*Sugar Loaf Mountain* towards north-east.
Parry House—with ruins of old mill in front.	*Beverly Dock*, close by river.
Buttermilk Falls, cascade above.	*Robinson House.*
Cozzens' Hotel, 250 ft above river, the most fashionable resort on the river.	*Hon. Hamilton Fish's Residence*, brick house on the bluff.
Highland Falls—village behind bluff. Population, 1,500.	*Garrison's*, 50 miles from New York, opposite West Point.
Cozzens' Landing.	*Highland House*, ½ mile from river, splendid site.
West Point, one mile above Cozzen's. U. S. Military Academy, Parade Ground, & Barracks. The most commanding point of the Hudson.	*Constitution Island*, opp. point.
Old Fort Putnam—ruins of the Revolution—598 feet above river.	*Miss Warner's* home, White Cottage, near the river. Author of "Queechy" and "Wide, Wide World."
Kosciusko's Monument, above West Point Landing, on the point.	*The Two Brothers*—rocks.
West Point Lighthouse.	*Cold Spring*, 54 miles from New York, with extensive iron foundries.
West Point Hotel, on the bluff.	*Undercliff*, home of George P. Morris, just north Cold Spring.
West Point Village.	*Mount Taurus*, 1,586 feet high.
Old Cro' Nest, 1,418 feet high.	*Little Stony Point*, promontory at foot of Bull Hill.
Kidd's Plug Cliff—the precipice on bank of river.	*Breakneck Mt.*, 1187 feet high.
Butter Hill.	*Beacon Hill*, 1,471 feet high.
Storm King, 1,529 feet high—highest point of the Highlands.	*Pollipel's Island*, at north entrance of the Highlands.
Cornwall Village, 56 m fr. N.Y.	*Duchess Junction.*
Idlewild, home of N. P. Willis, just north of Cornwall village.	*Fishkill Mountains* to the east.
Shawangunk Mountains west.	
New Windsor, four miles north of Cornwall.	

NEWBURG AND FISHKILL TO RHINEBECK.

WEST BANK.

Newburg Bay.

Washington's Headquarters— a flagstaff marks the location.

Newburg City, pop. 15,000, 60 miles from New York.

Duyvels Dans Kamer—flat rock covered with cedars—scene of the traditional Indian pow-wow which Hendrick Hudson and his comrades witnessed at night, with all its Indian accessories of fire and paint.

Hampton Point—with fine white cedars—64 miles from New York.

Marlborough, 66 miles from New York. The Arbor Vitæ grows in great perfection here.

Milton Ferry, or Barnegat, 71 from New York. Famous for the great quantity of raspberries raised in the vicinity.

New Paltz Landing, opposite Poughkeepsie, 75 miles from New York.

Large Ice Houses on the river-bank.

John Astor's summer residence.

Mr. Pell's great apple orchard, with 25,000 fruit-bearing trees.

Port Ewen, or Deserted Village.

Rondout, pop. 20,000, now City of Kingston. Terminus of extensive cement works.

EAST BANK.

Fishkill Landing, 60 miles from New York.

Low Point, or *Carthage,* 64 miles from New York.

New-Hamburg, 66 miles from New York, at the mouth of Wappinger's Creek.

Locust Point, country seat of the late Prof. S. F. B. Morse, inventor of electric telegraph.

Poughkeepsie Cemetery.

Ruins of Old Livingston Place just above.

City of Poughkeepsie, population 20,000, 75 miles from New York— Queen City of the Hudson, 200 feet above river.

River View Military Academy— brick building, on commanding site.

Vassar Female College is a mile and a half east of Poughkeepsie.

College Hill, north-east of city.

Poughkeepsie Water Works, in north part of the city, near river.

Hyde Park, 80 miles from New York. Named in honor of Gen. Edward F. Hyde, one of the early British Governors of New York.

Placentia, former home of the late James K. Paulding, one mile north of Hyde Park.

Dr. Hussack's Estate, with Corinthian pillars.

Esopus Island, 2 miles north of Hyde Park. On the rocks just below the Island the Steamer Berkshire was burned in 1864.

Stoatsburg, 85 miles from New York.

"*Wildercliff,*" built by Rev. Freeborn Garrettson.

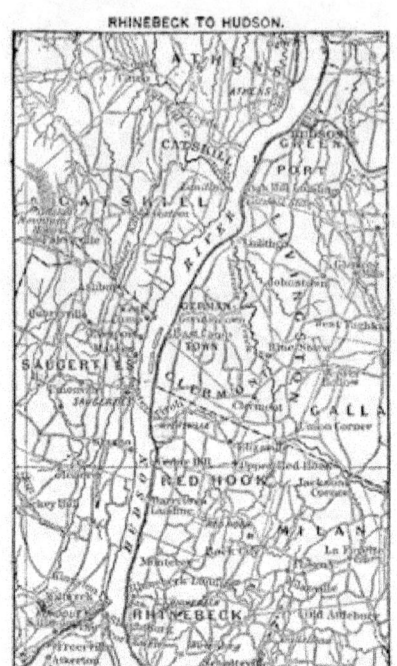

HUDSON RIVER.   xi

WEST BANK.

Glasgo.

Saugerties, pop. 5,000, at mouth of Esopus Creek.

Malden—with "Plattekill Clove" west.

Eversport, above Malden.

West Camp.

"*Four-County Island*"—junction of Dutchess, Columbia, Greene, and Ulster counties.

Catskill Mountains, 4,000 feet above the sea. Indian name, "*Onti Ora*," or "*Mountains of the Sky*."

Round Top, the highest peak of the Catskills, 4,000 feet above the river.

Catskill Mountain House, white building on the mountain, 3,000 feet above the river.

Catskill Village, 112 miles from New York. Pop. 4,000. Steam ferry connects with Catskill Station, 3 minutes in crossing.

Prospect Park Hotel, on bluff near the landing, 250 feet above the river.

Residence of John Breasted, Esq., proprietor of Prospect Park Hotel, second house north of hotel.

Athens, opp. Hudson. N. Y. Central R. R. Depot for freight near river, north of village.

EAST BANK.

Rhine Cliff, 90 miles from New York—with

Rhinebeck Village two miles east.

Barrytown, 96 miles from New York.

Rokeby, residence of William B. Astor.

Montgomery Place, 1 mile north of Barrytown, built by the widow of Gen. Richard Montgomery, who was killed at the storming of Quebec in 1775.

Cruger's Island, two miles north of Barrytown.

Tivoli, 100 miles from New York.

"*Claremont*," original Livingston Manor.

Germantown, 105 miles from New York.

Livingston, 109 miles from New York.

Catskill Station.

Church, the Artist, has a fine residence on the high point opposite Catskill.

Residence of John E. Gillette, Esq., nearer the river.

Rogers Island, behind which the shipping of the New York merchants was concealed during the Revolution.

Mount Merino, two miles above, just south of the

City of Hudson, 115 miles from New York, pop. 10,000. Extensive Iron Works near river. The Hudson and Boston R. R. terminates here.

HUDSON RIVER.

WEST BANK.

Four-Mile Point, 125 feet high.
Coxsachie, pop. 2,500, 123 miles from New York.
New Baltimore—here begin the government dykes.
Beeren, or *Bear Island*—meeting point of the four counties of Albany, Rensselaer, Columbia, and Greene—site of the "Castle of Rensselaerstein," from whose wall Nicholas Koorn, the agent of Killian Van Rensselaer, the Patroon, compelled passing vessels to dip their colors and pay tribute or take the chances of being sunk by the ordinance of the fort.
Coeyman's—Heiderberg Mountains to the west.
Shad Island, north of Coeyman's, three miles long—old Indian fishing ground.
Albany, 144 miles from New York. Pop. 70,000. Towards the south we see the buildings of the Convent of the Sacred Heart, Almshouse, and further north the Cathedral, State House, City Hall, etc. Two extensive R. R. bridges cross the river at this place. Both are over 4,000 feet in length.
Principal hotels are the Delavan and Stanwix Hall.

EAST BANK.

Stockport, four miles north of Hudson.
Newtown Hook and *Prospect Grove.*
Stuyvesant, formerly Kinderhook Landing.
Schodac Island, 8 miles long.
Schodac Village, opposite Coeyman's.
Nine-Mile Tree.
Castleton, 135 miles from New York.
Overslaugh, or *Castleton Bar,* extends about two miles up the river.
Extensive Dykes for several miles made by United States Government.
Campbell's Island—with Light on the south end.
Greenbush, or *East Albany,* connected with Albany by two fine railroad bridges.
Troy, six miles above Greenbush, 150 miles from New York. Population 50,000. Extensive Iron Works just south of the city. Seat of Rensselaer Polytechnic Institute.
Large building on the hill with four pointed towers is a Roman Catholic institution.

At Albany we leave the Steamer and take Rensselaer and Saratoga R. R. for Saratoga Springs. An Omnibus conveys passengers to the R. R. Depot.

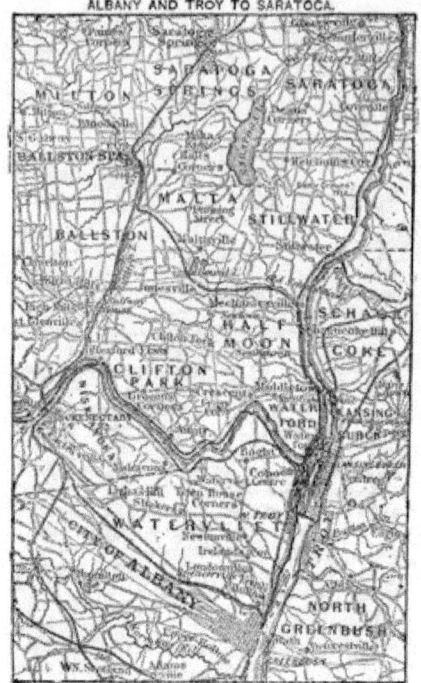
ALBANY AND TROY TO SARATOGA.

The Hudson River.

AMONG the thousand streams which drain the great Atlantic slope of North America, none is more attractive than the noble river at whose mouth stands the Empire City of the Western World. The magnificent bay through which it enters the ocean, the broad and deep waters which afford safe and easy navigation for large vessels a hundred and fifty miles inland, and the rich and beautiful country through which it flows, combine to render the Hudson River the most interesting among the streams of America.

The annually increasing army of tourists and pleasure-seekers which opens its campaign early every spring, and continues its march until late in the fall, sends every year a stronger corps of observation to the Hudson; and tourists find the great metropolis is the most agreeable and convenient starting point for their summer excursion. Nowhere can a traveling outfit be so advantageously procured; and a few days' sojourn amidst the whirl of business and fashion, which reaches its height just before the annual hegira to mountains, lakes, and forests, is usually a pleasant episode for pleasure-seekers of both sexes.

The European visiting America can have no better introduction to the Western Continent than that which is afforded by a voyage up the Hudson; and travelers generally will find that the river forms naturally the first stage of any extended pleasure-tour through the Northern and Eastern States.

SCENERY.

No change can be more charming than that from the glaring walls and pavements of New York to the sparkling waves and green banks of the river. In a few seconds, the traveler is transported from the dusty streets, with their deafening roar of traffic, to the broad river swept by the fresh sea-breeze, and stretching before him as far as the eye can reach, dotted with sails, sparkling in the sunlight, and bordered by scenery which is unrivaled by that of any other river on the Atlantic coast.

Scarcely has the traveler passed beyond the limits of the metropolis, when he is charmed by the green wooded hills of Westchester County on the one hand, and awed by the frowning precipices of the Palisades on the other. For twenty miles this mighty dyke of basaltic trap-rock shuts off the western sky, then suddenly disappears, and the view opens upon the rolling hills of Rockland County and the blue outline of the distant Ramapo Mountains; while on the east bank are thriving towns and elegant country-seats in almost continuous succession. Here, too, the river widens to the dimensions of a lake, which stretches its beautiful expanse nearly to the magnificent southern portal of the Highlands; there it suddenly contracts to a channel half a mile in width, overhung by the scarred and rugged crags of the *Donderberg* and *Anthony's Nose*. For twenty miles above, the river winds amid the grand and rugged mountains of "*The Highlands*," at whose northern limit another portal opens, through which the swift steamer carries us to new scenes of beauty beyond.

Above the Highlands the banks continue high, and in some places precipitous, opening now and then as if to afford glimpses of the charming country on either side, until some thirty miles more have passed before us like a beautiful panorama, when the banks become still less abrupt, and the lofty range of the Catskill Mountains comes in full view to the westward. Of these we speak more fully in another place.

In short, the steamboat trip by daylight between New York and Albany is one which every traveler should make. The river is everywhere rich in historical, legendary, and poetical associations, while the unsurpassed scenery and the constant evidences of commercial activity combine to render the trip one of ever-varying, never-ceasing interest.

TOPOGRAPHY.

The Hudson has its most remote sources among the highest peaks of the Adirondack Mountains, 4,000 feet above tide-water. Its numerous upper branches unite in the neighborhood of Fort Edward, 180 miles from the ocean, and thence follow a southerly course, broken by numerous falls and rapids, to Troy, where it meets tide-water. The remaining 150 miles are navigable by large steamers and coasting craft. Ships can ascend to Hudson. The principal tributaries are the *Mohawk* and *Hoosick* rivers, the former rising in the central part of New York, and the latter in southern Vermont, both joining the Hudson near Troy, below which city the tributaries, though numerous, are small, none of them being navigable for more than two miles.

The mountain-ranges through or near which the Hudson passes are part of the *Appalachian* system. The *Highlands* are a continuation of the *Blue Ridge*, which, after crossing Pennsylvania and New York, ends in the Green Mountains of Vermont and New Hampshire. The *Catsbergs* and *Hilderbergs* are continuations of the westward ranges of the *Alleghanies*.

The mean rise and fall of the tide at New York is about five feet, and at Albany two and a half feet.

GEOLOGY.

The geology of the Hudson is of so complex a nature that it is difficult in a few words to give even its general characteristics. In the nomenclature of State surveys, it is part of the "New York system," which corresponds to the Silurian and Devonian systems of European geologists. From the mouth of the river to the northern limit of the Highlands, the prevailing rocks are primary or igneous, such as granite and gneiss, containing no organic remains, but mixed, covered, and interstratified with shales, limestone, marble, serpentine, and sandstone; while the huge basaltic trap-dyke known as the *Palisades* rises like a wall along the river for twenty miles from its mouth, breaking up through the superincumbent strata of rock and drift, and forming a marked feature in the geological map, as in the landscape.

Above the Highlands the river flows through an extensive field of talco-argillaceous slate, which ranges from a gray color to almost black. In Dutchess County, veins of gold-bearing quartz are found injected into the cracks of this great slate system. Much of the drift of this region is formed of disintegrated slate. In Ulster County, water limestone is found in large quantities, and is very valuable for cement. Sandstone is found suitable for flagging. Further to the north the country is in ridges of sand or clay, mixed with slate in various stages of disintegration.

AGRICULTURE, ETC.

The river passes between the counties of Westchester

Bergen (N. J.), Rockland, Putnam, Orange, Dutchess, Ulster, Columbia, Greene, Rensselaer, and Albany. Of these, Rockland, Orange, and Dutchess counties may be mentioned as especially noted for the excellence of their dairy products. The two last-named of these counties are likewise famous breeding-places for trotting horses. The celebrated Hambletonian stock is cultivated with great care, and some of the fastest trotters in the world have been raised and trained on the farms of this region. In the other counties hay and grain are cultivated to a considerable extent, and in some portions of them apples, pears, and other fruits are raised in large quantities. Albany and Rensselaer counties are especially favorable to the cultivation of fruits, particularly plums, which are raised in great variety and perfection. The difference in temperature above and below the Highlands is very remarkable—fruits and cereals often reaching perfection at Peekskill two weeks in advance of the same crops at Newburg, twenty miles north. This difference is caused in great part by the sea-breeze, which is checked by the abrupt southern slope of the Highlands, leaving the region above open only to the colder breezes from the north.

COMMERCE.

The Hudson, during the season when it is not obstructed by ice, is the channel of extensive and increasing traffic. It is the natural outlet for lumber from the vast forests of the north. This lumber is floated down the main stream and its branches during the high water of early spring, and several millions of feet are every year brought to market in this manner. The *Delaware and Hudson Canal* brings vast quantities of coal from Pennsylvania, and keeps numerous barges constantly plying between its junction with the river at Rondout and the various cities reached by water from that point. The *Erie Canal*, connecting the Great Lakes with the ocean, through the Hudson River, affords means of transportation for Western produce and for the manufactured goods of the East. The immense "tows" of canal boats ascending and descending the river form an important and interesting feature of its commercial life.

Quarries of various kinds of stone, valuable for building, paving, flagging, etc., are found at various points on and near the river; and in Ulster County water limestone, making the best cement, is found in inexhaustible quantities.

Manufactories, founderies, machine-shops, ship-yards, and agricultural products unite to swell the numbers of every sort of vessel suitable for navigating these waters, and the fisheries afford employment and support to many men during the season for catching the different kinds of indigenous and migratory fish which inhabit the river and its tributaries.

During the winter, many thousand tons of ice are cut and stored for domestic use and for exportation to other lands.

HISTORY.

It is difficult to fancy a greater change than that which has taken place at the mouth and along the shores of the Hudson River within the past two and a half centuries. In September, 1609, when *Hendrick Hudson* and his sturdy crew sailed through the narrows, and anchored their yacht, the *Half-Moon*, in New York Bay, the shores were covered with a magnificent forest, unbroken save by natural meadows, or by the villages of Indians. The beautiful bay and river, now one of the busiest scenes of commercial activity in the world, were without signs of human life, except the few canoes of the natives; and Manhattan Island, with its dense population of a million souls, its splendid streets and buildings, and its proud commercial position as the Metropolis of the Western Continent, was a hilly, thickly wooded island, inhabited by a fierce and warlike race of savages.

Hendrick Hudson was sent out by the Dutch East India Company to search for a northwest passage to India, a problem which has tempted explorers even to our own day; and when he looked up the long line of the Palisades and noted the strong ebb and flow of the tidal currents at the mouth of the river, he thought his object gained. Accordingly he sailed up the river, viewing with wonder and delight the magnificent scenery, and observing the natural wealth of the country, until, on September 21, having reached the present site of Albany, he became convinced that he was following a river, and not a strait. He was everywhere received with great friendliness by the Indians; but when returning to the ocean, Hudson's mate shot an Indian for stealing, which caused an immediate collision, and several natives were killed.

Hudson returned to Europe, and in consequence of his reports, trading vessels were soon sent out, and after a few years of traffic in furs, a settlement was made in 1614, on the southern point of Manhattan Island.

During the Revolutionary War, the Hudson was the scene of constant activity on the part of both armies. Washington early perceived the strategic importance of the river and its dependencies, and used every means to retain possession. The British, however, in 1776, wrested Manhattan Island from our then inexperienced troops, and retained it during the war. They were unable to effect a permanent lodgment above the island, although they made several successful raids up the river, once reaching as far as Kingston. Fortifications were erected at various commanding points along the river, whose sites are pointed out in the following pages.

THE DAY LINE OF STEAMERS

Plying between New York and Albany possesses attractions and advantages which are seldom combined in one route of equal length.

The whole distance between the Metropolis of the Western Hemisphere and the capital of the Empire State is most remarkable for the beauty of its scenery, and for the evidences of commercial prosperity which greet the eye on every hand.

The boats of this line—namely, the well-known *C. Vibbard* and the *Daniel Drew*—are probably without exception the swiftest steamboats in the world. Built especially to meet the requirements of summer travelers on the Hudson River, these boats combine qualities of speed and comfort with facilities for viewing the magnificent scenery through which they pass.

To this end, while ample retiring-rooms are provided for ladies or invalids, the decks are unusually broad and open, so that an unobstructed view of the neighboring scenery may be obtained from almost any part of the boat. In order to meet the needs of persons who are unable to endure the strong breeze caused by the rapid motion of the boat, the forward saloons are provided with large windows, whence everything can be seen as well as from the more airy promenade decks.

Spacious and well-ventilated dining-saloons enable the traveler to take his meals in comfort and luxury, unannoyed by the usual accompaniments which ordinarily mark the dining-room of a steamboat as a sleeping apartment.

Travelers ascending the Hudson by rail, or at night, lose the extreme pleasure of this delightful trip. The cinders, smoke, noise, and fatigue of a railway journey need not be mentioned to the modern traveler; while the partial views obtained of river and mountains from a night boat serve but to suggest the charms of nature which only a trip by daylight can fully reveal.

The two boats are essentially the same in size and equipments. The dimensions of the *C. Vibbard* are as follows:

Length of keel.... 265 feet.	Diameter of cylinder.. 62 inches.
Breadth of beam,. 34 "	Length of stroke.... 12 feet.
Depth of hold.... 9 ft. 8 in.	

The highest speed ever attained by these boats was made by the *Vibbard*, which went from New York to Tarrytown, 27 miles, in one hour. The same boat also has run from West Point to Newburg (10 miles) in 20½ minutes. This speed was made on an extraordinary occasion, and it need not be expected that the powers of the boats will be so tested when loaded with passengers. The ordinary rate of speed is fully great enough to satisfy any reasonable traveler.

The boats leave Pier 39, North River, at the foot of Vestry Street, New York, at 8.10 o'clock A.M., touching 15 minutes later at 24th Street, and reaching Albany at 6 o'clock P.M., landing at the foot of the Canal Basin, whence they start on their return trips at 8.30 o'clock A.M., reaching New York at 6.00 o'clock P.M. To reach the foot of Vestry Street, New York, by horse-cars, take any of the up and down town lines, and request the conductor to let you off when he crosses the *Grand Street cross-town line*, which will land you at Pier 40, N. R.

To reach the foot of 24th Street, N. R., take the 10th Avenue line and get off at 23d Street, whence a short walk will take you to the wharf. Any *cross-town* line of cars will enable you to reach the 10th Avenue without walking.

The Route of the Hudson River.

JERSEY CITY AND HOBOKEN.

As the steamer leaves her wharf and turns her head to the northward, the panorama of river and bay opens before us. To the westward is *Jersey City*, merging into *Hoboken*, the limit of the latter place being marked by the rocky promontory long known as Castle Hill, on which stands the mansion of the Stevens family. In the vicinity of Hoboken are many elegant residences of wealthy New Yorkers, but the rapid increase of population is fast depriving them of the almost rural seclusion which they have until recently enjoyed, and the ornamental grounds which for a long time beautified the ridge back of the town are cut up into city lots.

On the east side of the river is New York, with its apparently interminable line of wharves and rows of warehouses, stretching northward as far as the eye can reach, and ending in a forest of masts towards the south, beyond which are the gray walls of Castle William on Governor's Island, and still further the waters of *New York Bay*, the *Narrows*, and *Staten Island*. The scene is always full of life and variety, and at certain times when wind and tide are favorable, the waters are alive with craft of all sizes, making for their various destinations all over the world, and seemingly in danger of constant collision.

WEEHAWKEN.

North Bergen, Bergen Co., N. J.

Between Hoboken and Weehawken are the *Elysian Fields*, formerly a beautiful park, but now retaining few traces of the rural walks which once made it a favorite resort of New Yorkers. It continues to be visited by large numbers of pleasure-seekers, but the attractions afforded by its noble trees and romantic grottoes have vanished, to make room for beer-gardens and places of entertainment. The Indian name was *Weehawk*, but custom has added the termination now invariably affixed. The scene of the duel between *Alexander Hamilton* and *Aaron Burr* is in Weehawken. The spot was formerly marked by a monument, but some reckless person destroyed it, and now but few are able to point out the place. It is a short distance above the point where a steep bank approaches the shore of the river. The fatal quarrel between these two prominent

THE STEAMER MARY POWELL ENTERING THE HIGHLANDS OF THE HUDSON RIVER.

men was a political one, and was marked by great malignity on the part of Burr, who took deadly aim, notwithstanding Hamilton's avowed purpose—which he carried out—of not returning his fire. Hamilton received a wound which proved fatal in a few days, and Burr was from that time almost ostracized, owing to the indignation of the public at what was esteemed a cold-blooded murder.

MANHATTANVILLE

Is a part of New York. The name is applied to the neighborhood of 132d Street. The conspicuous building on high ground, a little south of Manhattanville, is the *Lunatic Asylum*. It is surrounded by about forty acres of ornamental grounds, which are devoted to the use of the inmates of the Asylum. Nearer the river is the *Claremont Hotel*, where in former years lived *Viscount Courtenay*, afterwards *Earl of Devon*. *Joseph Bonaparte* occupied the house during the first year of his exile in this country. It is now a popular resort for frequenters of the Bloomingdale road.

CARMANSVILLE.

At 152d Street is another suburb of New York, and, being further from the city, contains more of the elements of a rural district. The distinguished naturalist *Audubon* lived here for many years, and is buried in *Trinity Cemetery* near-by. The large building surmounted by a dome a little above Carmansville is the *New York Institution for the Deaf and Dumb*. It stands on the southern slope of Washington Heights, commanding a wide view, and surrounded by spacious and cultivated grounds. The buildings are in the form of a quadrangle, and are capable of accommodating 450 pupils. The institution is the oldest of its kind in the country, excepting that at Hartford, Conn. It was incorporated April 15th, 1817.

FORT WASHINGTON.

10 *miles from New York.*

That portion of Manhattan Island known by the name of Washington Heights is the only part which retains to any great degree the natural attractions which formerly rendered the whole island so beautiful. The grading and leveling of city engineers has not yet reached this charming region, although it is penetrated by streets in every direction, and contains elegant residences throughout its whole extent. The fortification after which this place is named was an extensive earthwork occupying the crown of Washington Heights, and commanding the river above and below, as well as the neighboring country. It formed the end and citadel of an irregular line of works extending along the northern part of the island. The point extending into the river under Washington Heights is *Jeffrey's Hook*, and among its cedars are mounds which mark the site of a redoubt built at the same time with the neighboring fortifications. These works, with their garrison of 2,700 men, were captured by the British after a sharp resistance, on Nov. 15, 1776. This was the second defeat of the Americans in New York, and was a severe blow to the friends of the republic in this vicinity.

FORT LEE.

Hackensack, Bergen Co., N. J.
10 miles from New York.

The traveler is now opposite the lower end of the Palisades, which stretch in an unbroken wall of columnar trap-rock for 20 miles along the river. These rocks vary in height from 300 to 500 feet above the water, and are crowned by a heavy growth of timber. Houses are already beginning to be erected along the edge of this cliff, which commands a wide and beautiful view of the river and its shores, including Manhattan Island and the East River to Long Island Sound. Doubtless before many years a continuous line of villas will crown the top of this remarkable ridge. *Fort Lee* stood on the summit of the ridge at its southern extremity. A little village now occupies its site. The remains of the fort are scarcely discernible, and cannot be seen at all from the river. This fort was occupied by the Americans until after the British had captured Fort Washington in 1776, when it also was abandoned, and the Americans retreated across the State of New Jersey.

SPUYTEN DUYVIL.

New York City and Co.
12 miles from New York.

The cluster of houses on the upper side of the creek whose mouth is here seen, is known as *Spuyten Duyvil*, but the name was originally applied only to the creek itself, which connects Harlem River with the Hudson, thereby forming Manhattan Island. Through this estuary tide-water flows, the currents meeting at or near *King's-bridge*, about a mile from the Hudson.

The name *Spuyten Duyvil* is ascribed by the veracious Diedrich Knickerbocker (Washington Irving), to Anthony Van Corlear, the redoubtable Dutch trumpeter, who, being bound on an important mission to the mainland, and finding himself unable to procure a boat, swore that "*en spuyt den duyvil*" he would swim the creek. He plunged in, and when midway across was observed to struggle violently, until no longer able to resist the *Duyvil*, who was doubtless tugging at his legs, he raised his trumpet to his lips, gave a loud blast, and sank forever to the bottom. However it obtained its name, the vicinity is interesting. The creek formed the southern boundary of the famous *neutral ground* of revolutionary times, where the regular troops of the American and British armies were continually making raids. At Kingsbridge, redoubts were thrown up on both sides of the creek, and on December 19, 1780, an encounter took place between the Americans and a large detachment of British and Hessians, which led to no decisive result. Another skirmish occurred here in 1776, between a party of American stragglers and a Hessian guard, in which the former gained the advantage. Prior to these events, Hendrick Hudson and the Manhattan Indians had a long-sustained fight just at the mouth of the creek, where Hudson anchored the *Half-Moon*, in October, 1609. The Indians tried to board the yacht from their canoes, but were repulsed.

PALISADES MOUNTAIN HOUSE.
Englewood, Bergen Co., N. J.

Opposite Spuyten Duyvil is Lydecker Peak, the highest point of the Palisades, which projects somewhat into the river. Upon this peak stands the magnificent Palisades Mountain House, in full view from the railroad and river. It is one of the finest summer hotels on the Hudson, and owing to the charming scenery it commands, the beautiful drives about it, its nearness to New York, its ease of access, and the superb style in which it is kept, it is a very popular resort for New Yorkers. It is reached by steamboats from Harrison street, New York, to the dock at the foot of the Palisades, where stages await each boat, or by Northern N. J. R. R., from Chambers St. and W. 23d St., to Englewood, N. J. The house is kept by D. S. Hammond, a very popular proprietor.

RIVERDALE.
New York City and Co., 14 Miles from City Hall.

This village is composed almost entirely of the country residences of gentlemen doing business in New York. About a mile and a half above Riverdale is *Mt. St. Vincent*, a large educational institution, owned and controlled by the Roman Catholics. It is under the control of the Sisters of Charity, who purchased Font Hill, from the celebrated tragedian, Edwin Forrest. The castellated structure of dark stone was built by Forrest as a private residence. This building is now part

PALISADES MOUNTAIN HOUSE, ENGLEWOOD, N. J.
On the Hudson River opposite Spuyten Duyvil.

of the Mt. St. Vincent Academy, though, unfortunately, the two buildings are architecturally inharmonious.

YONKERS.
Yonkers, Westchester Co., N. Y.
17 miles from New York.

Yonkers is a flourishing town at the mouth of the *Neperah* or *Saw-Mill River*. The former name was given by the Indians, and signifies "rapid-water village," aptly describing the series of falls and rapids with which the stream joins the Hudson. The town is largely composed of the residences of city business men. Hendrick Hudson anchored off Yonkers when ascending the river in September, 1609, and was visited by large numbers of Indians with whom he traded. In the evening the tide set strongly up stream, which confirmed Hudson in the belief that he was in a passage between two oceans.

The name *Yonkers* is derived from the Dutch *Yonk-heer*, signifying the heir of a family.

The greater part of this region was purchased from the Van der Donck family, to whom it was originally granted by Frederick Philipse. The old *Philipse Manor* still exists, and is a most attractive object for those interested in relics of the olden time. The manor stands within the town of Yonkers. The older portion was built in 1682, and the more modern portion in 1745. It is probably the finest specimen of an old-fashioned mansion in the country. The interior decorations have been scrupulously preserved, and are very quaint and curious. In this old Hall was born Mary Philipse, the belle of her day and the early love of Washington. She chose to marry another, Roger Morris; but it is said that Washington always cherished the memory of the beautiful heiress of Philipse Manor.

HASTINGS.
Greenburg, Westchester Co., N. Y.
21 miles from New York.

About midway between Yonkers and Hastings, on the opposite side of the river, is the highest point of the Palisades, nearly 500 feet above the river. It is known as "Indian Head," and from it may be obtained a wide view over the neighboring country. Hastings is similar in its characteristics to Yonkers, and contains many beautiful country-seats. The country in its vicinity is diversified, and intersected by excellent roads, which render the rides and drives in every direction most attractive.

A British force, under Cornwallis, crossed the river at this place in 1776, joined another force in capturing Fort Lee, and then pur-

THE MEMORIAL FOUNTAIN, POUGHKEEPSIE, N.Y.
Erected by the Hon. H. G. Eastman.

GREGORY HOUSE, LAKE MAHOPAC, N. Y.,

Is situated fifty miles north of New York, on the Mahopac Branch of the Harlem Railroad. It is reached from New York or from the North on the Harlem Railroad, Grand Central Depot, 42d St. and Fourth Ave. Passengers leave the main line of that road at Golden's Bridge, and a ride of twenty minutes brings them to the Mahopac Depot, which is about a half mile from the Lake. Stages connect with every train.

Lake Mahopac is the largest of the many lakes in this vicinity. It covers 1200 acres, and is 900 feet above tide-water. The boating privileges are not excelled; and the drives in the vicinity are far more beautiful than those that are found at most other watering places. On the border of the Lake, south of the hotel, is a neat cottage containing three good Billiard-Tables and four Bowling Alleys. The Livery Stables, Billiard and Bowling Halls, Boats, etc., are all under my control, and I hold myself responsible for the good management of everything connected with the hotel. To the old patrons of the Gregory House no further assurance of satisfactory management will be needed. To the public generally, I would say, that no pains or expense have been spared to make this long-established and favorite summer resort as perfect in all its appointments as either acid taste could suggest. All possible precautions have been taken to secure the health and comfort of guests; the proprietor confidently looks for a continuance of the patronage with which the House has been favored for so many years.

L. M. GREGORY, Lake Mahopac, N. Y.

ed the Americans to the Delaware River.

DOBBS' FERRY.
Greenburg, Westchester Co., N. Y.
22 miles from New York.

A village of considerable size, containing villas and cottages of tasteful and elegant appearance. The village is named after a ferry which was kept in olden times between this place and Piermont opposite, by one Dobbs, a Swede. An attempt was made some years since to have this name changed to "*Paulding,*" as being both more euphonious and appropriate. The proposition led to quite a controversy in the newspapers; but public opinion decided, for the time at least, in favor of the old Swedish ferryman. The river here widens into *Tappan Bay,* or as it was called by the Dutch, *Tapaan Zee.* This bay extends to Croton Point, having an average width of nearly four miles.

Dobbs' Ferry is well known in Revolutionary annals. The British concentrated their forces here after their dearly bought victory at White Plains, five miles east. This battle took place in October, 1776.

In 1777 a division of the American army, under General Lincoln, was encamped here for several months. The Commission sent by Sir Henry Clinton to intercede for the life of the unfortunate spy Major André, landed here and held a long but unsuccessful consultation with General Greene, the president of the court which condemned him to death. Greene met the Chief of the Commission by permission of General Washington, only in the character of a private gentleman; but although both friend and foe desired to save André's life, the conference proved unavailing. Dobbs' Ferry was the first place appointed for a meeting between André and Arnold. The plan, however, was not successfully carried out.

PIERMONT.
Orangetown, Rockland County, N. Y.
24 miles from New York.

A short distance below Piermont is the line between New York and New Jersey, near which the Palisades recede from the shore and lose their precipitous character. The ridge continues, however, in a series of hills reaching, in some places, a height of nearly 700 feet, but nowhere resuming the peculiar palisade formation. The long pier which projects into the river from this place is the terminus of a branch of the Erie Railway, which connects with the main line at Suffern, 18 miles west. Two miles back of Piermont is Tappan, where, on October 2d, 1780, Major André was tried, condemned, and executed. (See page 22.)

IRVINGTON,

Greenburg, Westchester County, N. Y., 24 miles from New York,

Is a village of comparatively recent growth, inhabited in great part by the families of gentlemen whose places of business are in New York. The village is named in honor of *Washington Irving*, the genial author whose pen has done so much to preserve whatever is interesting in the traditionary history of the Hudson River. "*Sunnyside*," the home of Irving during the last years of his life, is a little north of the village, and glimpses of the picturesque house and grounds may be caught from the steamer as it passes. This house, with its quaint Dutch gables, includes the original building known to readers of Irving's works as "Wolfert's Roost," where Ichabod Crane courted the lovely Katrina Van Tassel, as related in the "Legend of Sleepy Hollow." Irving died November 28th, 1859, and was buried in the cemetery near Tarrytown, in that very "Sleepy Hollow" which his graceful pen has made forever famous.

TARRYTOWN.

Greenburg and Mt. Pleasant, Westchester Co., N. Y. 29 miles from New York.

Tarrytown is delightfully situated on a hillside overlooking the river and the Palisades to the southward, and commanding a distant view of the Ramapo Mountains and the Hudson Highlands to the west and north.

The whole town is thickly studded with dwellings of every size and every style of beauty. Prominent among these is the white marble edifice known as Paulding Manor, which stands just below the town. It was built by descendants of Commodore Paulding, and is one of the finest specimens of the Elizabethan style of architecture in this country. It has passed out of the possession of the Paulding family.

A little above Tarrytown is the *Pocantico*, a small stream flowing through the valley, called by the Dutch *Sleeperigh Haven*, and translated into English as *Sleepy Hollow*. About half a mile from the mouth of this stream is an old Dutch church, which is a curiosity in its way. It is the oldest church edifice in the State of New York, having been built in 1699. Its walls contain bricks which were imported from Holland when the church was erected. The old bell still hangs in the belfry, on whose pointed roof an iron vane still turns, bearing the monogram of the founder of the church, Frederick Philipse, whose mansion, known as *Philipse Castle*, stands on the banks of the stream not far distant. This is the dwelling whence the Philipse family moved when the mansion at Yonkers was built.

To the eastward of the church is the valley of Sleepy Hollow, and the identical bridge, or at least its successor, over which the Headless Hessian pursued Ichabod Crane, as related by Irving in the "Legend of Sleepy Hollow." Between this bridge and Tarrytown the road crosses *André's Brook*, and near by stands a monument marking the spot where he was captured. A suitable inscription gives the leading facts connected with that event.

THE PALISADES.

ANDRE AND ARNOLD.

THE story of Arnold's treason and of André's capture and execution is one of the most interesting in our history, and we will briefly recount the leading facts concerning it.

Benedict Arnold was, at the time of his treason, a major-general in the American army, having won his position by distinguished gallantry and zeal in the cause of the republic. It is not necessary here to trace the successive steps which led to his fall. Suffice it to say that certain acts of his while in command at Philadelphia led to his trial by court-martial. He was merely sentenced to be reprimanded, but the sentence, mild as it was, embittered him towards his country, and he soon began to take steps towards opening a correspondence with the enemy. He succeeded in getting himself assigned to the command of West Point and vicinity, and under the name of "Gustavus" began negotiations for the surrender of West Point with Sir Henry Clinton, then commanding the British forces which held New York. Finally arrangements were made for a meeting with *Major John André*, Adjutant-General of the British army. The first appointment was not kept, but a second was more successful. The British sloop of war *Vulture* was sent up to Teller's Point with André on board. Nothing occurred the first night; but the second night Arnold sent a small-boat, in which André was brought ashore. The boat landed on the west side of the river, at the mouth of Haverstraw Creek, just below Stony Point, and Arnold and André consulted together until daylight. Their plans were incomplete when day broke, and Arnold persuaded his companion to go with him to a tory house near by. Horses were at hand, provided by Arnold, and they rode together through the dark woods. Presently they were challenged by a sentry, and then André perceived that he was within the enemy's line—a spy. They went on, however, and entered the house. As soon as daylight was sufficiently clear, an American gun opened fire on the Vulture from Teller's Point, and the vessel weighed anchor and dropped down the river. André was in uniform, but in order to provide against discovery he put on a plain coat. In the course of the day plans for the surrender of the garrisons about West Point were completed, and André was anxious to regain the British lines. Being unable to get a boat to take him down to the Vulture, André was forced to take the land route. Accordingly he crossed King's Ferry from Stony to Verplanck's Point, passed through the American works at the latter, and, guided by a tory named Smith, and a negro servant, proceeded down the Tarrytown road. Arnold had given the party all necessary passes, so that American guards only halted the party temporarily. Reaching the last outpost the officer on duty persuaded them to remain all night, owing to the danger from marauders on the road further south. Early in the morning they went on. André's guide, accompanied him as far as Croton River, and there left him to go on alone. No regular American patrols went south of this river, but on this particular morning a party of volunteers had agreed to guard the road, and three of them were stationed at the brook near Sleepy Hollow. André soon appeared, and although he tried to disarm their suspicions, they compelled him to dismount and submit to a search. In his stockings were found the fatal papers. André offered bribes to a large amount if they would let him go, but the stern patriots refused his highest offers, and marched him off to the nearest American post. The commanding officer, Colonel Jamieson, was very near sending prisoner, papers, and all to Arnold, but Major Tallmadge persuaded him to send only a letter detailing the circumstances of the arrest. This letter Arnold received while at breakfast. He immediately left the table, ordered his horse, saying that he was wanted down the river, rode to Beverly Dock (see page   ), and leaping into his six-oared barge went down the river with all speed to the Vulture.

André at once wrote to Washington, frankly telling the whole truth about his complicity with Arnold, and closing with the words "Thus was I betrayed (being Adjutant-General of the British army) into the vile condition of an enemy in disguise within your posts." Washington convened a court, which tried André at Tappan. The accused so freely and truthfully admitted all the charges and specifications, that it was not necessary to examine a single witness, and the Court, after long deliberation, reluctantly sentenced him to death. Much sympathy was felt for André throughout the American camp, but every one acknowledged that under the circumstances no leniency should be shown. An informal proposition was made to exchange him for Arnold, but neither Washington nor Sir Henry Clinton would officially consider this plan, and on October 2. 1780, André was hung.

In 1832 his remains were removed to England, and a monument stands in Westminster Abbey on which the sad story is inscribed. Arnold was made a Major-General in the British army, and received £10,000, the price of his treason, but was despised even by his brother officers, and died with hardly a friend to mourn his loss. Monuments have been erected to the memory of Paulding and Van Wart, two of the men engaged in **André's capture at Peekskill and Tarrytown.**

NYACK.

Orangetown, Rockland Co., N. Y.
27 *miles from New York.*

Nearly opposite Tarrytown, at the foot of a precipitous hill. Red sandstone was formerly quarried in large quantities near this place, but the discovery of equally good stone nearer the river has rendered it unprofitable to work the mines.

SING SING.

Ossining, Westchester Co., N. Y.
32 *miles from New York.*

This town is on the east bank, and a large part of its houses command an extensive view down the river. Sing Sing is best known as the site of the State Prison, to which most of the convicts of New York City are sent. The white prison buildings will be readily recognized at the lower end of the town. The marble of which these buildings are constructed is the kind known as dolomite. It is quarried near by, and the prisons have been built by the convicts themselves. The main building was ready for occupation in 1829, but has received improvements and additions since. In connection with the prison, the name of *Capt. Elam Lynds* should not be forgotten. This officer took charge of a party of one hundred convicts at Auburn, brought them to Sing Sing (there were no railroads in those days), and set them to work to wall themselves in, which in due time was accomplished, and thus Sing Sing prison was begun. Capt. Lynds was a natural disciplinarian, and is said to have brought the hundred men from Auburn with the aid of only a few guards.

Opposite Sing Sing is a high hill, projecting somewhat into the river. This is known by its old Dutch name of *Verdritege Hook*. The name signifies "grievous," and was given in consequence of the frequent squalls which beset the sailor in this neighborhood. *Rockland Lake* lies on one of the shoulders of this mountain. This lake is about half a mile from the river, and 300 feet above it. Large quantities of ice are cut from its surface every winter. The slide by which the ice is sent down to be loaded on barges may be seen near the landing, leading straight up the hillside to the lake shore. The peculiar sharp-pointed peak near by is known as the *High Torn*.

TELLER'S AND CROTON POINTS.

Cortland, Westchester Co., N. Y.
36 *miles from New York.*

The extremity of this tongue of land, projecting far into the river from its eastern bank, is known as

Teller's Point. Croton Point is that portion nearer the shore of the river. It separates Tappan Bay from *Haverstraw Bay*. Off this point the Vulture anchored when she brought André to meet Arnold, and from thence the gun was brought to bear which drove that vessel down the river. Croton Point is now occupied by the vineyards of Dr. Underhill, whose pure wines are much used for medicinal purposes.

Just below Teller's Point is the mouth of *Croton River*, which supplies New York with water. This stream has a wide mouth, sometimes called *Croton Bay*, which was partly filled up in 1841 by the washing away of the Croton Reservoir dam. The work was, however, pressed forward, and in 1842 water was supplied to the city through the Croton pipes. The aqueduct is built of solid masonry, and follows the course of the Hudson at an average distance of about a mile from its shore. This aqueduct is capable of discharging 60,000,000 gallons per day into the receiving reservoir in the Central Park, New York. The entire cost of the Croton works at their completion was about $14,000,000. Since that time great improvements and additions have been made, to meet the demands of the growing city. It is estimated that the Croton River will supply water enough for New York even if the city should reach five times its present size.

HAVERSTRAW.

Haverstraw, Rockland Co., N. Y.

36 miles from New York.

For a few miles below Haverstraw, the summits of the Highlands are distinctly in sight, up the river, although their bases are hidden by intervening hills. The long ridge-like elevation, toward which the boat heads, is the *Donderberg*, near 1,000 feet in height. *Haverstraw* is the village seen on a high bank, or plateau, on the west side of the river, which above Croton Point spreads out into the wide and beautiful expanse known as *Haverstraw Bay*.

VERPLANCK'S POINT AND STONY POINT.

38 miles from New York.

These two points mark the upper end of Haverstraw Bay. *Stony Point* is on the west side of the river, a bold rocky eminence, having a lighthouse on its summit. Opposite, on the east side of the river, is *Verplanck's Point*, which may be recognized by several large brick-making establishments, with their kilns and drying-houses. Just below Stony Point is *Grassy Point*, and opposite to it *Montrosse's Point*. Between Stony and Verplanck's Point the river is only half a mile wide, which fact, together with the commanding positions afforded by the neighboring hills, rendered this an important pass during the Revolutionary War. Long previous to that war a ferry was established here known as *King's Ferry*, forming an important avenue of communication between the Eastern and Middle States. The importance of the Hudson River as a base of operations and as a natural boundary was early recognized by Washington, and here, as at Washington Heights, fortifications were erected commanding the river.

A short distance southwest of Stony Point is *Treason Hill*, whereon stands Smith's house, in which André and Arnold completed their scheme for the surrender of West Point, and whence André started to cross King's Ferry, on his fatal journey toward New York.

Above Stony Point a high limestone cliff rises from near the water's edge. At its foot are the "Tompkins Lime Kilns," looking like a stone fortress with arched casemates. These quarries have been worked for many years, and vast quantities of slaked lime are annually shipped to market. Besides the lime, between 30,000 and 40,000 tons of gravel, too coarse for slaking, are used for roads in the Central Park, New York, and other public highways in the vicinity.

The Capture of Stony Point.

The forts located at Stony Point were held by the Americans until June 1st, 1779, when they were simultaneously invested by a British force, commanded by Sir Henry Clinton. No direct attack was made on Fort Lafayette, the work on Verplanck's Point, until after the evacuation of Stony Point. The garrison at the latter place numbered only 40 men, and abandoned the work on the approach of an overwhelming force of the British, who quietly took possession, ran up the cross of St. George on the flagstaff, and opened fire on Fort Lafayette with the captured guns. At the same time Gen. Vaughan attacked on the east side of the river, and the weak garrison of 70 men was soon forced to surrender. The loss of this position was a severe blow to the Americans, compelling them to make a wide détour in order to keep up their communications. *General Anthony Wayne* at once requested and obtained permission to storm Stony Point, and at midnight on the 15th of July, 1779, led two columns of picked men to the assault. They advanced undiscovered until they were close upon the British picket, which of course gave the alarm, and the garrison turned out. The parapet was manned, and a scathing fire of grape and musketry swept the hillside; but "Mad Anthony" was at the head of his column, and, within half an hour after the first shot, carried the works at the bayonet's point, capturing the entire garrison with its stores. Wayne was knocked over, but not seriously injured, by a musket ball. The next morning a cannonade was opened on the works at Verplanck's Point, and continued through the day. Re-enforcements were sent to the British, and it soon became evident that sufficient force to hold Stony Point could not be spared by the Americans. They therefore dismantled and abandoned the fort, and it passed again into British hands. They, however, in turn abandoned the position in October, and from that time the Americans retained possession.

PEEKSKILL.

Courtland, Westchester Co., N. Y.
43 miles from New York.

Soon after rounding Verplanck's Point, Peekskill may be seen near the Highlands, on the east bank of the river. At this point, in ascending the river, a stranger naturally infers that the river follows the base of the high hills stretching to the eastward. This delusion is aided by the wide creek or inlet which opens in that direction. It will not therefore be thought strange that in early times *Jan Peek*, a Dutch skipper, steered his craft up this creek and in due time ran her hard and fast aground. Jan looked about him, and seeing that the land was good, concluded to remain, which he accordingly did, and the place is called *Peek's Kill* unto this day. The village is a pleasant one, and within easy reach of all interesting parts of the Highlands. The *Rev. Henry Ward Beecher* has a country residence a little east of the village.

Fort Independence stood, during Revolutionary times, on the point above Peekskill, where its ruins may still be seen.

The village on the point opposite Peekskill is *Caldwell's Landing*, and above it rise the rocky and weather-beaten crags of the *Donderberg*, or Thunder-mountain, around which, at the close of a sultry summer day, black clouds are wont to gather, casting a deep inky blackness over mountain and river, while mutterings of thunder are echoed from peak to peak, with such strange and confused rumblings that we can hardly wonder at the superstitions which, according to Irving, peopled the hills with a crowd of little imps in sugar-loaf hats and short doublets, who were seen at various times "tumbling head over heels in the rack and mist," and bringing down frightful squalls on such craft as failed to drop the peaks of their mainsails in salute to the Dutch goblin who kept the Donderberg. As the boat passes Peekskill the view up stream becomes truly magnificent. On the east shore opposite, and a little above the Donderberg, is *Anthony's Nose*, over 1,200 feet high. In the "History of New York," Irving gives an amusing account, too long to quote here, of the origin of this name. Another, and perhaps more trustworthy account, says that it was once jocularly compared to the nose of one Anthony Hogans, the captain of a sloop, who possessed an unusually large nose, and thus the name obtained a local currency which eventually became fixed as the title of this majestic hill. On the west side of the river is Iona Island, on which are extensive vineyards. This island is the northernmost point which is reached by the sea-breeze. The effect upon vegetation is very noticeable in the spring of the year.

The stream which may be seen falling into the river below Anthony's Nose is known as *Brocken K'ill*. It is full of romantic cascades, almost from its mouth to its source.

FORTS CLINTON AND MONTGOMERY.

Cornwall, Orange Co., N. Y.

47 miles from New York.

On the west side of the river, nearly opposite to Anthony's Nose, may be seen the mouth of *Montgomery Creek*. On the rocky heights above and below the creek stood Forts Clinton and Montgomery, which were in 1777 the principal defences of the Hudson. They were considered impregnable to an assault from the land side, and with the ordnance of the day they had little to fear from a naval attack. A heavy boom, made of a huge iron chain on timber floats, stretched across the river, and was made fast to the rocks at Anthony's Nose. This, it was thought, would effectually prevent the ascent of a hostile fleet.

On October 6th, 1777, Sir Henry Clinton sent a strong detachment around and over the Donderberg to attack these forts in the rear. A demonstration on the east side of the river had led General Putnam to anticipate an attack on Fort Independence, near Peekskill, and a portion of the garrison at Fort Montgomery was temporarily withdrawn to strengthen that post. The British had a sharp skirmish with an American detachment at *Lake Sinnipink*, which is still known among the inhabitants as "Bloody Pond." This attack was the first warning which aroused the garrison at the forts. In the course of the afternoon the forts were attacked, and the garrisons defended themselves gallantly until evening, when, it having become evident that they could not hold out, they took to the mountains, an orderly retreat being impossible, and so the greater part escaped. An American flotilla, consisting of two sloops and some smaller craft, which lay above the boom, had to be abandoned and burned to prevent its falling into the enemy's hands. The next morning the boom, which had cost the Americans so much labor and money, was destroyed, and the British fleet, with a detachment of troops, proceeded up the river. A short time afterwards the British received the news of Burgoyne's surrender, and the forts were evacuated.

Near Montgomery Creek another smaller stream falls into the Hudson. This is *Sinnipink Creek*, having its rise in a lake of the same name, half a mile distant. At the mouth of this stream is an ice depot of the Knickerbocker Ice Company. The ice is slid down from Sinnipink Lake on ways, and stored or summer use.

WEST POINT *(Landing).*
Cornwall, Orange Co., N. Y.
51 miles from New York.

Soon after passing the former site of Fort Montgomery, the gray ruins of Fort Putnam may be seen crowning the heights above West Point. A little cove may now be seen in the east bank of the river, where is a stone wharf, and two or three small buildings. This is "Beverly Dock," from which Arnold started in his hasty flight to the Vulture, which lay in Tappan Bay. On the hill, not far distant, is Robinson's house, where Arnold was breakfasting when he received the news of André's capture. Nearly opposite, and a little above Beverly Dock, *Buttermilk Falls* may be seen, breaking in snow-white foam over a black sloping rock. A considerable village stands on the stream above the fall. *Cozzens' Hotel,* a favorite and fashionable resort during the summer months, is on a commanding height near the falls. This hotel is surrounded on all sides by the most charming walks and pleasure-grounds.

West Point is best known as the site of the *United States Military Academy.* Before the commencement of the present century, Washington suggested this place as a proper one for the establishment of such an institution, but no formal steps were taken by Congress until 1802. Ten years later, in 1812, the school was fairly established, and has ever since continued to increase in importance and excellence.

But little of the academy can be seen from a passing boat, the buildings being situated on an elevated plateau, about 180 feet above the river. This plateau is occupied by the various barracks, schools, arsenals, etc., connected with the institution. These are so arranged as to leave a broad parade open for military evolutions, parades, etc.

The average number of cadets is about 250. Candidates for admission are nominated by members of Congress and by the President, a certain number being fixed for each congressional district. These candidates report for examination in June of each year, and, if they are mentally and physically qualified, are admitted as cadets, which is, in military rank, a grade below second lieutenant. The course of instruction is very thorough and complete, especially in mathematics; military tactics and operations bearing an important place. The best time to visit West Point is during the months of July and August, when the cadets go into camp. Drills, parades, and guard-mountings are the order of the day, all being done in the best manner known in military science.

West Point was the scene of no actual fighting during the Revolution, although it was fortified. A boom similar to that which was prepared at Fort Montgomery was stretched across the river from West Point to *Constitution Island*. The island was heavily fortified toward the latter part of the war, and remains of the old batteries may still be seen. Of the fortifications on the west side of the river Fort Putnam is the most interesting. It is 596 feet above the river, and the view from its crumbling walls is exceedingly fine.

INDIAN FALLS, GARRISON, N. Y.

GARRISON.
Philipstown, Putnam Co., N. Y.
50 Miles from New York.
HOTEL—*Highland House.*

This station, named in honor of a distinguished family of Revolutionary fame, is on the east bank of the Hudson, opposite West Point. It is surrounded by the most sublime and picturesque scenery of the Hudson, and is associated with some of the eventful scenes of Revolutionary times. About one mile south of the depot is the Robinson House, where Benedict Arnold received the

(VIEW IN THE GROUNDS OF EASTMAN PARK, POUGHKEEPSIE, N. Y.

COZZENS' HOTEL.—*Cozzens' Landing, West Point, N. Y.*
GOODSELL BROTHERS, *Proprietors.*

This elegant and favorite summer resort stands on a commanding eminence on the west side of the Hudson, 250 feet above the river, and about one mile and a half south of the Military Academy of West Point. It commands one of the finest views on the Hudson, embracing the very heart of the Highlands, and the wildest and most picturesque scenery on this famous river. Its location is remarkably healthful; no cases of sickness having originated at this resort in twenty-five years. West Point was selected as the site of the Military Academy partly because of the healthfulness of the locality. Its location is particularly convenient for New York families, as it is but fifty miles distant, and gentlemen are enabled to visit New York daily, returning to Cozzens' at night if they desire. Among the many places of interest around Cozzens' are the U. S. Military Academy, where daily military exercises of interest occur, old Fort Putnam, Beverly Dock, Robinson House, Buttermilk Falls, etc. The drives among the historic Highlands are celebrated for their enchanting beauty, and one or two, including the five-mile drive to Crystal Lake, have recently been laid out. Distinguished visitors, including our national officials and celebrities, annually visit West Point Academy during the examinations, which begin on the 1st of June.

The hotel is built of brick, and is so constructed that all its rooms command delightful views of the river and mountain scenery. It will accommodate about 400 guests, who are the most refined and respected classes of our metropolitan society. The house is kept in a style to suit such patronage, and Cozzens' Hotel stands unrivaled among our summer resorts in its quiet elegance and comfort.

The table is not surpassed by any hotel in America in luxuries or style, and excellent music daily enlivens the enjoyments of this elegant and unexceptional resort. It can be reached by the Hudson River Railway to Garrison's Station, whence a steam-ferry conveys passengers to Cozzens' Dock; or by Day Line Steamers to West Point, with omnibus to Cozzens' Hotel, or the Mary Powell and Jas. W. Baldwin to Cozzens'. Carriages await at Cozzens' Dock and West Point the arrival of all boats and trains. Daily excursions may be made from New York, stopping for dinner and spending three or four hours at the hotel, returning to the city the same day. Passengers should not mistake the West Point or Government Hotel for Cozzens', but drive to *Cozzens' Hotel*, kept by *Goodsell Bros.*

HUDSON RIVER AT WEST POINT, LOOKING SOUTH.
COZZEN'S HOTEL, IN THE DISTANCE.

letter from Col. Jamieson, informing him of the arrest of André. These noted historic places are easily visited from the Highland House, situated about half a mile east of the R.R. station, on a plateau commanding one of the most delightful prospects for which the banks of the Hudson are so justly celebrated. It is surrounded on the east and south with mountains abounding in running brooks and wild, shaded glens, while it overlooks West Point and the Highlands to the west. The house is so situated as to receive the cool breezes from the west and north which circulate on the eastern side of the valley of the Hudson. The hotel is conducted by the Messrs. Garrison, descendants of the family from which the place derives its name, and is in all respects a well-conducted resort. In the vicinity are delightful drives and places of peculiar beauty, among which are Indian Falls, Glen Falls, North and South Redoubt, Anthony's Nose, and Sugar Loaf Mountains on the east side of the river; and West Point, Fort Putnam, Old Cro' Nest, Storm King, Highland Falls on the west side; while the beautiful Hudson, bright with many a sail and steamer, flows majestically through the mountains toward its ocean home. Altogether, it is one of the most delightful resorts to be found in America. **Near by** are the summer residences of Hon. Hamilton Fish, Secretary of State of the United States, and several other prominent citizens of New York City.

COLD SPRING.

Philipstown, Putnam Co., N. Y.

54 miles from New York.

Cold Spring is noted for its Iron Foundry. Here, under the superintendence of Major Parrot, were cast the celebrated Parrot guns, which did such good service in the war of the Rebellion. On an elevated plateau near the village is *Undercliff*, the country-seat of the late *George P. Morris*. The mountain immediately above Cold Spring is *Bull Hill*, or, to give its more classic name, *Mt. Taurus*. It is 1,586 feet in height. Just above this elevation, and separated from it by a valley, is *Breakneck Hill*, 1,187 feet high. It is stated that the former of these hills was once the abode of a wild bull, which became such a source of dread to the inhabitants that they organized a hunt, and drove the animal from his accustomed haunts across the valley to the neighboring hill, where he dashed over the rocks and broke his neck. The two hills were named in honor of this adventure. *Breakneck Hill* was formerly dis-

HIGHLAND HOUSE, GARRISON'S, N. Y.

Situated immediately in the Highlands of the Hudson, 200 feet above the river directly opposite to and **Commanding a Full View of West Point**, being of higher ground in the midst of the Mountains, one-half mile back from the Mansion on the Hill, **Supplied With Pure Spring Water**. The Lawn is fifteen acres in extent and abundantly filled with Shade Trees, giving ample play-ground, making it one of the finest, if not the **Best Family Hotel on the Hudson**. Horses and Carriages, Billiards and Bowling Alleys connected with the House. **All Trains stop at Garrison's**, and the Steamboat Mary Powell, Vibbard and Daniel Drew land at West Point, and passengers cross the river to Garrison's by steam ferry. Direct access to West Point Parade Grounds by stage and steam ferry. In twenty minutes' time from the House. Address, or call at Grand Union Hotel, (Foemm) Park Avenue, 41st Street, NEW YORK CITY, where Diagram of the Rooms can be had.

G. T. & W. D. GARRISON, Proprietors.

THE RESIDENCE AND PLEASURE GROUNDS OF HON. H. G. EASTMAN, PRESIDENT
OF EASTMAN COLLEGE, POUGHKEEPSIE, N. Y.

This beautiful private Park, one of the finest in this country, has never been closed by a gate, but has been for years, as free to the public as though it was the property of the city.

tinguished by a huge mass of rock, bearing a marked resemblance to a human face. This singular formation was for many years one of the sights to be looked at by every passenger up or down the river. In 1846 a party of workmen was blasting near by, under the charge of a Captain Ayers, and an unfortunate blast loosened the rock, so that *St. Anthony's Face*, as it was called, was forever destroyed. Mr. Blake accuses Ayers of intentionally causing this mutilation of the mountain, but we are loth to believe that such could have been the case. The face was on the southwestern angle of the mountain, and the wreck of fallen rocks may still be seen from the passing boat.

The promontory at the foot of Bull Hill is known as *Little Stony Point*.

On the west side of the river are *Cro' Nest* and *Butter Hill*. The former is the one next above West Point. It is 1,418 feet high, and separated from Butter Hill by a wild and picturesque valley. The name *Cro' Nest* probably was at first applied to a deep rocky depression which exists near the summit, but it is now understood to mean the mountain itself. The name will recall *Joseph Rodman Drake's* beautiful poem, "*The Culprit Fay*," the scene of which is laid among these hills.

The precipice which forms the river-face of Cro' Nest is known as "*Kidd's Plug Cliff*." It owes its name to a singular projecting mass of rock which may be seen near its summit.

The neighboring mountain has of late come to be called the *Storm King*, and as the old name is neither beautiful nor appropriate, it will soon be forgotten. Its summit is 1,529 feet high. To the late *N. P. Willis* is due the credit of rechristening this grand peak, as well as giving appropriate names to other objects of interest in the vicinity. Mr. Willis' cottage, "*Idlewild*," stands almost on the northern slope of the Storm King, and commands extensive views of the neighboring country. The cottage itself can hardly be seen from the river.

CORNWALL LANDING.

Cornwall, Orange Co., N. Y.
56 miles from New York.

The village of Cornwall is a short distance west of the river. The beauty of its situation renders it a fashionable resort during the summer, when its many beautiful residences are the scene of a constant round of gayety.

After passing Breakneck Hill, *Beacon Hill* may be seen to the eastward. This elevation is 1,471 feet in height, and commands a prospect which has given it considerable

THE NEWBURGH INSTITUTE.

Seminary Place, NEWBURGH, N. Y.

HENRY W. SIGLAR, A.M. (Yale); JOHN MATHIE, A.M., *Principals*.

THE NEWBURGH INSTITUTE occupies the buildings and grounds widely known as the *Seminary Place*, situated in the suburbs of the city and sufficiently removed from the troublesome influences of business centres. Two substantial stone buildings, one four stories and 70x40 feet, and the other two stories and 25x40 feet, furnish abundant first-class accommodations, while the grounds, containing three acres, afford ample room for outdoor sports. The position is a commanding one—overlooking the City of Newburgh and the Hudson for many miles.

The Institute is a *Family School for Boys*, conducted, in respect to its boarding arrangements, on the plan of a well-ordered home. The pupils reside with Mr. Siglar, where they are regarded as actual members of his family. In fact, all the affairs of the household are regulated with special reference to the comfort, health, moral culture, and refinement of the boys connected with it. The pupils are not partitioned off by themselves, but they share in the best that the house affords, join the family circle, and enjoy the social advantages of a Christian home.

The Plan of the School is such that boys may begin their school-life at the Institute, and there receive a thorough preparation for College, or as extended an education as may be desired, preparatory to entering upon a business or a professional life.

The Elementary Branches of an English education are taught with the greatest care and thoroughness. The constant aim is to make thinkers as well as scholars, to teach self-control and self-reliance.

For INFORMATION in regard to the Institute as a Preparatory School, parents are referred to the Faculty of Yale College; in regard to the thoroughness with which the elementary branches are taught—to former pupils, now in business, and to patrons.

The Course of Study aims at a thorough mastery of a few subjects, in preference to a showy and superficial acquaintance with a number of studies for which no foundation has been laid. Pupils intended to follow a collegiate course, are carefully prepared for entrance to any of our colleges—our success in this department has been very gratifying. Pupils intended for business life, are specially grounded in the studies most essentially important to a business man.

The Twelfth Annual Session will begin on TUESDAY, September 14th, 1875. With the exception of short recesses at Christmas and Easter, the session will continue without interruption till July 1st, 1876. The TERMS for Board, Washing (12 pieces per week), and Tuition in all studies, are $400 per annum; $200, to be paid at the beginning of the session, and $200 on the 1st of February.

Circulars sent on application to the Principals.

point, and shipped by water to various destinations.

A flag-staff, standing in the southern part of the town, may be seen from the steamer. Near this is an old stone house, now owned and kept in order by the State, which was occupied by Washington as his headquarters when the army lay at New Windsor, two miles south. This house contains many interesting relics of the Revolutionary War. At the foot of the flag-staff before mentioned, the last surviving member of Washington's Life Guard was buried in 1856, and a monument, with an appropriate inscription, stands over his grave.

A short distance south of Newburg is the site of the American camp where, during the winter of 1783, the troops suffered so severely from the attacks of smallpox.

The Newburgh Institute is an excellent and well-established boarding-school for boys. The building is a large stone structure, overlooking the city, and commanding a view of some of the finest scenery of the Hudson.

LOW POINT.

Fishkill, Dutchess Co., N. Y.

64 miles from New York.

This is a small village on the east bank of the Hudson. Opposite, on the west bank, is a flat rock, now crowned with cedars, which Hendrick Hudson and his comrades named the *Duyvels Dans Kamer*, in consequence of an Indian pow-wow which they witnessed at night, with all its hideous accessories of fire and war-paint. The rock is still known to the river pilots by this name.

NEW HAMBURG,

Poughkeepsie, Dutchess Co., N. Y.,

66 miles from New York,

Stands at the mouth of *Wappinger's Creek*, which falls into the Hudson on the east side. This stream is crossed at its mouth by a long trestle bridge, with a draw in the middle. A ferry plies between New Hamburg and Hampton opposite.

MARLBOROUGH.

Marlborough, Ulster Co., N. Y.,

66 miles from New York,

Is pleasantly situated on the west bank of the Hudson, overlooking the river and the country beyond. Back of the village are the Shawangunk Mountains, and intervening is a hilly country of great beauty. In this vicinity the *Arbor Vitæ* is found in great perfection. This tree is also known as the white cedar. Its scientific name is *Thurja Occidentalis*. A peculiarly beautiful grove of these trees will be noticed on the west bank, a little above Marlborough, where an entire hillside is covered with the delicate pencil-like

MILTON FERRY or BARNEGAT.
Poughkeepsie, Dutchess Co., N. Y.
71 *miles from New York.*

The village, or part of it, may be seen crowning the steep bank which rises from the western shore of the river. Large quantities of raspberries are raised in this vicinity for the New York market, the soil and climate being peculiarly adapted to the cultivation of that fruit.

Just before reaching Poughkeepsie, which city may be seen on the bluff beyond, we pass *Locust Grove*, the country-seat of *Prof. S. F. B. Morse*. It can hardly be necessary to remind any civilized being that Prof. Morse is the inventor of the electric telegraph, now so indispensable to every nation of Christendom. The professor has made other useful inventions, and had in his earlier life a reputation as an artist. His fame, however, rests on the discovery of the electric telegraph, and for this he has received many testimonials from European sovereigns, and from scientific associations all over the world.

POUGHKEEPSIE.
Poughkeepsie, Dutchess Co., N. Y.
75 *miles from New York.*

The city of Poughkeepsie is built on a table-land, at a considerable height, so that its spires and buildings may be seen from a long distance up and down the river. The name is a corruption of the Indian name given to the cove which once existed at the mouth of *Fall Kill*. Two peculiar elevations will be noticed at the river-side, the southern of which bears the name of *Call Rock*, from the fact that the inhabitants used to hail passing vessels from its summit. The place was settled by the Dutch about 1698, and incorporated as a city in 1854. The principal object of interest to the antiquary is the Van Kleek house, a stone structure with loop-holes in its walls. It was built in 1705. The State Legislature met in it in 1777 and 1778, when the British held New York, and had burned their former meeting-place at Esopus. There also the State Convention for the ratification of the Federal Constitution met, in 1788. 57 members were present, and after a long debate, in which such men as Governor Clinton, John Jay, and Alexander Hamilton took part, the Constitution was ratified by a majority of three.

Poughkeepsie is the shire town of Dutchess County, and contains, the usual court and jail buildings. The streets of the city are beautifully shaded, its situation is very healthful, and everything combines to make it most attractive as a residence. The *Vassar Female Col-*

POUGHKEEPSIE, N. Y.—THE CITY OF SCHOOLS AND BEAUTIFUL RESIDENCES.
The Location of Eastman Business College.

THE BALDWIN HOUSE,

NEWBURGH, ORANGE CO., N. Y.

This new and elegant hotel has just been completed and handsomely furnished throughout, and is now open for the reception of guests. It is situated on an eminence overlooking the city, 200 feet above tide-water, and commands a view of the *Hudson River* and adjacent country, which for beauty, variety and extent cannot be surpassed. THE BALDWIN HOUSE is provided with all the modern improvements and conveniences for guests, and is kept open all the year round. The surrounding country abounds in the most delightful walks and drives, and the river below affords ample opportunity for boating, sailing and fishing. It may be reached from New York via the Erie R. R. from Chambers or West 23d St. ; via Hudson River R. R. from Grand Central Depot, 42d St. and 4th Av., or via the "Day Line" Steamers from Pier 39, foot of Vestry St., for Newburgh, at 8 A. M. The Mary Powell leaves same pier at 3.30 P. M., and the Steamers J. W. Baldwin and Thomas Cornell leave pier foot of Harrison St. at 4 P. M. Time from New York to Newburgh 2 hours. Passengers leaving New York via Day Line Steamers in the morning may have two hours for dinner in Newburgh and reach New York via the same line at 6 P. M.

For further particulars address the proprietor, Mrs. J. T. COCKS, Baldwin House, Newburgh, N. Y.

lege is the largest and most important of the many excellent educational institutions of Poughkeepsie. The late *Matthew Vassar*, a wealthy citizen of Poughkeepsie, founded and endowed this extensive college. It is intended for the education of women only, and is the most complete establishment of its kind in the world.

NEW PALTZ.
Lloyd, Ulster Co., N. Y.
75 miles from New York.

This village is the shipping point for the farm produce of the rich agricultural region to the westward. Ice is cut from the Hudson in considerable quantities, and stored for use in the large buildings on the river-bank.

HYDE PARK.
Hyde Park, Dutchess Co., N. Y.
80 miles from New York.

Named in honor of Sir Edward Hyde, one of the early British Governors of New York. The village is half a mile east of the river-bank, on a beautiful and fertile table-land. The bend in the river between rocky bluffs is known to river men as *Crum Elbow*, a combination of the original Dutch name and its English equivalent. A creek of the same name falls into the river. The point on the east shore is *De Vries Point*. A light iron foot-bridge will be noticed crossing a deep cut-ting of the Hudson River Railroad. The house beyond is that of *Joseph Boorman*, first President of the Hudson River Railroad.

Between Hyde Park and Oak Hill, 30 miles above, there is a large number of extensive and ancient country-seats, many of them antedating the Revolution. The beauty of the country seems to have attracted men of taste and wealth in those days to make their homes along this fertile bluff, and in many cases their descendants still occupy the old mansions of their fathers,—a state of things so rare in America as to deserve especial notice.

About a mile above Hyde Park landing is "*Placentia*," the former home of the late *James K. Paulding*, one of the pioneers of American literature, and the friend of Washington Irving. Opposite, on the west bank, but scarcely in sight from the river, is the famous apple farm of *R. L. Pell, Esq.* On this farm there are said to be 25,000 bearing apple-trees. The fruit of these trees is packed with the greatest care, and much of it is shipped to Europe.

STAATSBURG.
Hyde Park, Dutchess County, N. Y.
85 miles from New York.

The banks of the river from this place northward lose the precipitous character which has marked them thus far, and slope from the river in a less abrupt manner. Two miles above Hyde Park, *Esopus Island* will be noticed near the east bank. Just below it are some low rocks, on which the steamer *Berkshire* was burned in 1864. She caught fire off the island, and was purposely run on these rocks to enable the passengers to escape. Just below Esopus Island, on the west side of the river, is the residence of John Astor, Esq. Opposite are two fine estates, the lower owned by Dr. Hussack, and the upper by Mrs. M. Livingston.

The village of *Stantsburg* is on the east bank.

RONDOUT.

Kingston, Ulster County, N. Y.
90 *miles from New York.*
HOTEL—*Rhinecliff House.*

Rondout Creek enters the Hudson from the westward. Its mouth is the eastern end of the Delaware and Hudson Canal, which joins the creek 2½ miles above. This canal, finished in 1828, extends to the vicinity of the Pennsylvania coalfields; and every provision is made at Rondout for the trans-shipment of vast quantities of coal.

PORT EWEN

Is a comparatively new village, below the mouth of the creek. Nearly all the inhabitants of these villages are engaged in one way or another in the coal business, and in the extensive Rosendale cement quarries, whose products are highly valued, and largely used all over the country.

KINGSTON,

Formerly *Esopus*, is on *Esopus Creek*, which at that point approaches within about 2 miles of Rondout, and then curves to the northward, entering the Hudson 12 miles above. Kingston was settled in 1614, and was thrice destroyed by Indians before a permanent footing was obtained by the Europeans. In 1777 the State Legislature met and formed a constitution. In the autumn of the same year, soon after the capture of Forts Montgomery and Clinton by the British, General Vaughan, with 3,000 troops, landed at Rondout, marched to Kingston (then Esopus), and sacked and burned the town, remaining until they received the news of Burgoyne's surrender, when they at once retired to New York, abandoning all that they had gained. While Esopus (Kingston) was burning, the inhabitants fled to Hurley, a neighboring village, where the small force of American troops tried and hung a messenger who was caught carrying dispatches from Clinton to Burgoyne. When first caught

ij a silver ball, sought again to as found to contain.

BECK.

*n County, N. Y.
New York.*
zatsburg, on the r, is the country-*Idercliff.* It is gant as many of states; but to ethodist Church cresting as haveborn Garrett-preacher, who Chancellor Livne energy is due sperity of that ristian Church, a recognised by ich lies in front jext above this the residence of n *Kelly,* long al life. His es-fion acres, much ed to gardens ounds, and the rated as a farm. use on a hill near ; is the Beekman r to 1700. It i and as a fort , when the In-wl powerful. Rhinebeck is 2 miles from the river, and cannot be seen from the steamer. Within the limits of the town there is an extensive vein of gold-bearing quartz, which yields the precious metal in paying quantities. The principal lode is on the property of R. W. Millbank, but it probably extends to and beyond the river. This quartz is found between well-defined walls of the ordinary talco-argillaceous slate characteristic of the region.

BARRYTOWN.

Red Hook, Dutchess County, N. Y.
96 *miles from New York.*

Formerly known as *Lower Red Hook Landing.* A little above Rhinebeck is the residence of *William B. Astor.* It may be recognised by its tower and pointed roof. This estate is named *Rokeby,* and is one of the finest on the river. Next above is the estate known as *Montgomery Place,* surpassing in beauty, if possible, the last one mentioned. The house was built by the wife of General Montgomery, who fell in the assault on Quebec in 1775. Her brother, Edward Livingston, succeeded her in the ownership of the place, and his family still occupies it.

Near the eastern shore, 2 miles above Barrytown, is Cruger's Island, a spot made beautiful by **nature** and art.

In a grove near the southern end stands a ruin which was imported from Italy by the former proprietor of the island. Its broken arches may be seen among the trees as the boat passes, forming a singular contrast with the modern architecture of the neighboring house. The latter, however, is not in sight from the boat at the same time with the ruin. A glimpse of it may be caught in passing, a short distance above.

TIVOLI.
Red Hook, Dutchess Co., N. Y.
100 *miles from New York.*

This is a small village around the railway station. Near the village is an old mansion now owned by Col. De Peyster, which was built before the Revolution by one of the Livingston family. The British, on their way to burn Claremont, a little above, in 1777, stopped here, under the impression that this was the house to be destroyed. The proprietor, however, aided by his well-stocked wine-cellar, convinced them of their mistake, and they left him unmolested.

SAUGERTIES.
Saugerties, Ulster Co., N. Y.
100 *miles from New York.*

Saugerties is near the mouth of *Esopus Creek*, which is navigable to the village. There are extensive iron works and paper-mills at this place, and large quantities of flagging-stone are quarried in the vicinity. A short distance above Saugerties is Malden.

"Plattekill Clove," which lies back of this place, in the mountains, is a remarkably wild and rugged chasm, affording scenery of varied grandeur and beauty. A road winds through this gorge up to the mountain region beyond. Passing the landings of East and West Camps we soon reach

GERMANTOWN.
Germantown, Columbia Co., N. Y.
105 *miles from New York.*

The view of the Catskill Mountains is here very fine. The entire range can be seen, and the *Catskill Mountain House* may be distinguished in relief against the sky.

Germantown is not directly upon the river-bank, and cannot be seen from the boat. The large white building on a hill near the landing is the *Riverside Seminary*, established by Philip Rockafellow.

A few miles above Germantown is the mouth of *Roeleff Jansen Kill*, where the original Livingston Manor House stood. *Robert R. Livingston*, Chancellor of New York, built an elegant house, a little south of the old one, where his mother continued to reside. Chancellor Livingston's active sympathy with the cause of the Republic during the Revolution made him so obnoxious to the British, that when Gen. Vaughan burned Esopus he sent an expedition up the river to burn Claremont—the name of the Livingston estate. They burned both the houses, but new and more elegant ones were at once erected near the ruins, and Claremont is still one of the finest country-seats on the river. Chancellor Livingston's name will always be associated with that of *Robert Fulton.*

The experiments of the latter in applying the steam-engine as a motive power for boats would probably have been delayed for years had it not been for the generous aid of Chancellor Livingston. After a series of discouraging failures in Paris and New York, their efforts were crowned with success, and in September, 1807, the "*Claremont*" made her first trip from New York to Albany, bearing Fulton and the Chancellor, as well as a party of invited guests.

CATSKILL.

Catskill, Greene Co., N. Y.
111 *miles from New York.*
HOTELS—*Prospect Park House; Irving House.*

Catskill Landing is at the end of a long causeway, reaching across the shallows, on the western shore. But little of the town can be seen from the river. *Cats Kill* enters the Hudson near by, winding through rocky bluffs, with a deep channel, which is navigable for large vessels a mile from its mouth. Travelers intending to visit *The Catskill Mountains* can reach their destination most easily from this point, as lines of stages run regularly to the Mountain House, 8 miles distant. For a particular description of the mountains see page .

Hendrick Hudson anchored the *Half-Moon* at the mouth of Cats Kill, on the 20th of September, 1609, and was visited by large numbers of friendly Indians, who brought provisions of all sorts, in return for which, as is stated by Juet, the historian of Hudson's voyage, some of them were made drunk.

Thomas Cole, one of the pioneers of American Landscape Art, had his studio in this vicinity, where he could study nature in her most beautiful forms. It was here that he painted the celebrated allegorical series of pictures known as "The Voyage of Life."

The country between the river near Catskill and the mountains is very interesting to the geologist, comprising as it does the exposed strata of all the principal rocks of the so-called New York system.

PROSPECT PARK HOTEL,
CATSKILL, N. Y.

A NEW SUMMER HOTEL.

A well situated, well arranged, and well conducted Place of Resort, of easy access, on the banks of the Hudson River.

WITH ALL THE LATEST IMPROVEMENTS.

The House has been greatly enlarged this season. The main building is two hundred and fifty feet front by forty feet; with wing one hundred and forty by forty feet. Dining-room full length of wing. With two-story Piazza, three hundred and seventy by sixteen feet.

The grounds, walks, avenues, and shrubbery are adapted to the chief design, which is, to produce such an establishment, on a liberal and appropriate scale, as can offer to those, who with their families annually seek the country during the Summer months, health and grateful change from the heat and confinement of the city.

THE VIEWS FROM THE HOTEL ARE UNSURPASSED IN EXTENT AND BEAUTY.

The annually increasing tide of visitors to this region—drawn hither by the pursuit of health and pleasure—has already vindicated its right to the title of "the Switzerland of America."

The locality is a judicious selection from the Prospect Hill property, in the Village of Catskill; and the site, with its surroundings, occupies twenty acres. The plateau is admirably adapted to the purpose. With a commanding view of the River in front and for miles North and South, and the grand old Mountains in the background, with a climate of great salubrity, healthy mountain air, and accessories of field and river sports and pleasant drives, it is unsurpassed, in all the borders of the Hudson, for its attractions and advantages.

☞ Carriages will be in attendance at the Cars and Boats.

Accessible by nearly all Trains of the Hudson River Rail Road, and by the Day Boats "*Chauncey Vibbard,*" "*Daniel Drew.*" Also by Night Steamers "*New Champion*" and "*Andrew Harder,*" every evening, from foot of Franklin Street, New York.

☞ First-class Livery connected with the Hotel.

WILL OPEN JUNE 14th.

Address **JOHN BREASTED, Catskill.**

CATSKILL MOUNTAIN HOUSE

1824.   53rd Season.   1876.

CATSKILL MOUNTAIN HOUSE.—Largest Hotel in the Catskill region, only first-class House on the Mountains, and the only one commanding the famous view of the Hudson Valley. Open June 1st to October 1st. Send for circular. C. L. BEACH, Catskill, N. Y. CATSKILL AND MOUNTAIN HOUSE STAGES AND CARRIAGES.—An Agent in attendance on the arrival of all Trains and Boats at Catskill.
CHAS. A. BEACH, Proprietor.

The Catskill Mountains.

HOTELS.—*Mountain House, Laurel House,* **Haines' House**.

The mountain scenery bordering upon the Hudson is justly celebrated for its diversity and beauty; nor is this region less interesting to the man of science than to the tourist in search of the picturesque and beautiful.

The mountains of this region all belong to the great Appalachian range, which traverses the eastern portion of the United States, from the States bordering on the Gulf of Mexico to the basin of the St. Lawrence River. The chain is made up of a succession of ridges whose prevailing course is parallel with each other and with the general coast line of the continent.

The general character of the Appalachian range in New York is a gradual change from mountains to hills, which finally sink away in the lowlands of the great St. Lawrence basin. Three distinct ranges or collections of parallel ridges pass through New York State, from South west to North-east.

The first or most easterly of these is the continuation of the great Blue Ridge of Virginia, Maryland, and Pennsylvania, the main portions of which, passing through the North-western corner of New Jersey, forms the Shawangunk Mountain, which, extending between Sullivan and Orange counties, strikes the Hudson in the southern part of Ulster county. South-east of this long ridge a succession of smaller ridges run parallel with it, some of which cross Orange and Rockland into Putnam and Dutchess counties, east of the river. The gap through which the Hudson flows is across these smaller ridges, whose highest summits rise to heights varying from one thousand to seventeen hundred feet above tide-water. The Taconic and Green Mountains of Western Massachusetts and Vermont are probably prolongations of the Blue Ridge.

The second series of these ridges enters the State from Pennsylvania, and extending through Sullivan, Ulster, and Greene counties, terminate in the beautiful Catskills, a short distance west of the Hudson.

The third series, passing through Broome, Delaware, Otsego, Schoharie, Montgomery and Herkimer counties, reappears beyond the Mohawk, and there constitutes the Adirondac Mountains, among whose summits the Hudson finds its sources.

The following sketch of the scenery of the Catskill region is taken by permission from a work entitled

THE CATSKILL MOUNTAINS, AND THE REGION AROUND; their Scenery, Legends, and History. By Rev. CHARLES ROCKWELL, Dutch Dominie of the Catskills, etc., etc. *New York: Taintor Brothers & Co., Publishers*, 229 Broadway. 1867.

"From the banks of the Hudson, a few miles into the country, may be seen, from different points of view, some of the most charming scenery in the world. Every turn in the road, every bend in the stream, presents new and attractive pictures, remarkable for beauty and diversity in outline, color, and aerial perspective. The solemn Katzbergs, sublime in form, and mysterious in their dim, incomprehensible, and ever-changing aspect, almost always form a prominent feature in the landscape.

"The Indians called these mountains "Onti Ora," or "Mountains of the Sky;" for, in some conditions of the atmosphere, they are said to appear like a heavy cumulose cloud above the horizon. In the midst of this scenery, Cole, the eminent painter, delighted to linger when the shadows of the early morning were projected towards the mountains, then bathed in purple mists; or at evening, when these lofty heights, then dark and awful, cast their deep shadows over more than half of the country below between their bases and the river. Charmed with Catskill and its vicinity, Cole made it at first a summer retreat, and finally his permanent residence; and there, in a fine old family mansion, delightfully situated to command a full view of the mountains and the intervening country, his spirit passed from earth; while a sacred poem, created by his wealthy imagination and deep religious sentiment, was finding expression upon his easel in a series of fine pictures like those of "The Course of Empire" and the "Voyage of Life." He entitled the series "The Cross and the World." Two of them were unfinished. One had found form in a "study" only, while the other was half finished upon the large canvas, with some figures sketched in white chalk. So they remain, just as the master left them; and so remains his studio. It is regarded by his devoted widow as a place too sacred for the common gaze. The stranger never enters it.

The mountains rise abruptly from the plain on their eastern side, where the road that leads to the Mountain House enters them, and follows the margin of a deep, dark glen, through which flows a clear mountain stream, seldom seen by the traveller, but heard continually for nearly a mile, as in swift rapids or in little cascades it hurries to the plain below. The road is winding, and in its ascent along the side of the glen, or, more properly, magnificent gorge, it is so inclosed by the towering heights on one side, and the lofty trees that shoot up on the other, that little can be seen beyond a few rods except the sky above or glimpses of some distant summit, until the pleasant nook in the mountain is reached wherein the Rip Van Winkle cabin is nestled. After that the course of the road is more nearly parallel with the river and the plain, and through frequent vistas glimpses may be caught of the country below that charm the eye, excite the fancy and imagination, and make the heart throb quicker and stronger with pleasurable emotions. Rip's cabin is a small, white building, with two rooms, where travellers formerly obtained refreshments; and is at the head of the gorge along whose margin the traveller has ascended. It is so called because it stands within the amphitheatre, inclosed by lofty heights, reputed to be the place where the ghostly ninepin players held their revel; and where Rip Van Winkle lay down to his long repose. From a rude spout by the cabin there pour cooling draughts from a mountain spring, more delicious than ever came from the juice of the grape.

There are many delightful resting-places upon the road, soon after leaving Rip's cabin, as we toil wearily up the mountain, where the eye takes in a magnificent panorama of hill and valley, forest and river, hamlet and village, and thousands of broad acres, where herds graze and the farmer gathers his crops; much of it dimly defined because of distance, a beautifully colored map rather than a picture. These delight the eye and quicken the pulse; but there is one place upon the road where the ascending weary ones enjoy more exquisite pleasure, for a moment, than at any other point in all that mountain region. It is at a turn in the road where the Mountain House stands; suddenly, before and above the traveller, revealed in perfect distinctness, column, capital, window, rock, people,—all apparently only a few rods distant. There too the road is level, and the traveller rejoices in the assurance that the toilsome journey is at an end, when suddenly, like the young pilgrim in Cole's "Voyage of Life," he finds himself disappointed in his course. The road that seemed to be leading directly to that beautiful mansion upon the crag just

THE FAWN'S LEAP.

THE LAUREL HOUSE,
AT THE CAUTERSKILL FALLS,

Catskill Mountains, 1½ mile West of Mountain House.

J. L. SCHUTT, Proprietor.

The great beauty of this locality is so well known, that a description is unnecessary. To the lovers of quiet, its secluded walks afford delightful retreats; while the drives in the vicinity—especially through the Clove—challenge comparison with any similar place in the United States. There is also good Trout Fishing in the neighborhood.

A wing 50x50 feet has been added to the House recently, greatly extending the accommodations at this popular resort.

Carriages and an authorized Agent will be in attendance at the Cars and Boats, Catskill.

above him turns away, like the stream that appeared to be taking the ambitious young man directly to the shadowy temple of fame in the clouds; and many a weary step must be taken over a steep, crooked road before the traveler can reach the object of his journey.

The grand rock platform on which the Mountain House stands is reached at last, and then comes the full recompense for all weariness. Bathed, immersed, in pure mountain air, almost three thousand feet above tidewater, full, positive, enduring rest is given to every muscle, after half an hour's respiration of that invigorating atmosphere, and soul and limb are ready for a longer, loftier, and more rugged ascent. There is something indescribable in the pleasure experienced during the first hour passed upon the piazza of the Mountain House, gazing upon the scene towards the east. That view has been described a thousand times. I shall not attempt it. Much rhetoric and rhyme, with sentimental platitudes, have been employed in describing it.

The aerial pictures seen from the Mountain House are sometimes marvellous, especially during a shower in the plain, when all is sunshine above, while the lightning plays and the thunder rolls far below those upon the summits; or after a storm, when mists are driving over the mountains, struggling with the wind and sun, or dissolving in the pure air. At rare intervals an apparition, like the spectre of the Brocken, may be seen. A late writer, who was there during a summer storm, was favored with the sight. The guests were in the parlor when it was announced that "the house was going past, on the outside." All rushed to the piazza; and there, sure enough, upon a moving cloud more dense than the fog that enveloped the mountains, was a perfect picture of the great building, in colossal proportions. The mass of vapor was passing slowly from north to south, directly in front, at a distance apparently of two hundred feet from the house, and reflected the noble Corinthian columns which ornament the front of the building, every window, and all the spectators. The cloud moved on, and ere ong we saw one pillar disappear, and then another. We, ourselves, who were expanded into giants in size, saw the gulf into which we were to enter and be lost. I almost shuddered when my turn came; but there was no escaping my fate; one side of my face was veiled, and in a moment the whole had passed like a dream. An instant before, and we were the inhabitants of a gorgeous palace; but it was the "baseless fabric of a vision," and now there was left "not a wreck behind."

Although the Mountain House is far below the higher summits of the range, yet portions of four States of the Union and an area of about ten thousand square miles are comprised in the scope of vision from its piazza. From the top of the South Mountain, near and three hundred feet above the Mountain House, and of the North Mountain more distant and higher, a greater range of sight may be obtained, including part of a fifth State. The lakes, lying in a basin a short distance from the Mountain House, with all their grand surroundings, the house itself, the South Mountain, and the Roundtop or Liberty Cap, form the middle ground; while in the dim distance the winding Hudson, with Esopus, Shawangunk, and the Highland ranges are revealed, the borders of rivers dotted with villas and towns, appearing mere white specks on the landscape.

Two miles and a half from the Mountain House is an immense gorge scooped from the rugged hills, into which pours the gentle outlet of the Cauterskill Lakes, in a fall, first of one hundred and seventy-five feet, and close to it another of eighty feet. If the visitor would enjoy one of the wildest and most romantic rambles in the world, let him follow that little stream in its way off the mountains, down the deep, dark, mysterious gorge, until it joins the Cauterskill proper, that rushes through the Clove from the neighborhood of Hunter, among the hills above, and thence onward to the plain. The tourist, if he fails to traverse the rugged gorge, should not omit a ride from the Mountain House, down through the Clove, to Palensville and the plain, a distance of eight miles. After leaving the falls and reaching the Clove, down, down, sometimes with only a narrow space between the base of a high mountain on one side and steep precipices on the other, whose feet are washed by the rushing Cauterskill, our crooked road pursued its way, now passing a log house, now a pleasant cottage, and at length the ruins of a leather-manufacturing village, deserted because the bark upon the hills around, used for tanning, is exhausted.

Near this picturesque scene the Cauterskill leaps into a seething gulf between the cleft rocks and flows gently on, to make still greater plunges into darker depths a short distance below. This cleft is called the "Fawn's Leap," a young deer having there escaped a hunter and his dog, that pursued to the verge of the chasm. The fawn leaped it; but the dog, attempting to follow, fell into the gulf below and was drowned. The foiled hunter went home without dog or game. By some, less poetical than others, the place is called the "Dog Hole." A few rods below the Fawn's Leap the road crosses a rustic bridge, at the foot of a sheer precipice, and for half a mile traverses a shelf cut from the mountain side, two hundred feet above the stream that has found its way into depths so dark as to be hardly visible. Upon the opposite side of the creek, a perpendicular wall rises many hundred feet; and then, in

slight inclination, the mountain towers up at least a thousand feet higher, and forms a portion of the range known
as the South Mountain. At the mouth of this cavernous
gorge lies the pretty little village of Palensville, where we
again cross the stream, and in a few moments find ourselves upon a beautiful and highly cultivated plain. From
this point, along the base of the mountains to the road
by which we enter them, or more directly to Catskill, the
drive is a delightful one.

DELAVAN HOUSE,
ALBANY, N. Y.
CHARLES E. LELAND & CO., Proprietors.

THIS HOTEL WAS BUILT IN 1871, AND IS SITUATED ON THE

MAIN STREET,

And in the centre of the village.

IT IS FITTED UP WITH NEW FURNITURE

And all the

Modern Conveniences of First-class Hotels,

And the Proprietor assures the Public that no efforts on his part will be spared to make his guests comfortable.

COACHES TO THE MOUNTAIN HOUSE

And all other

STAGE LINES RUNNING FROM CATSKILL.

Stop for passengers at this House.

An OMNIBUS runs to and from the Hotel on arrival of Trains and Steamboats.

H. A. PERSON,

Proprietor.

HUDSON.

Hudson, Columbia County, N. Y.
115 *miles from New York.*
HOTELS—*Worth House, Mansion House.*

The City of Hudson is the capital of Columbia County, and occupies a site of great beauty, being built upon a promontory jutting into the Hudson River, and commanding the most extensive and charming views in every direction. The city extends up the slope of Prospect Hill, which rises to a height of 200 feet. The elevation just below Hudson Landing is *Mount Merino*. It is cultivated over almost its whole surface of 600 acres. Hudson, being at the head of ship navigation, was of great importance in the early commerce of the river, and it rapidly grew to be a place of considerable size and wealth. The Claverack Creek, a romantic stream, is a little east of Hudson, and running northward, joins other streams, forming *Columbiaville Creek.*

The *Hudson and Boston Railway* has its western terminus here, and connects at *Chatham* with the *Boston and Albany and Harlem Railways.*

ATHENS.

Athens, Greene County, N. Y.
115 *miles from New York.*

This village, directly opposite Hudson, was originally fixed upon as the eastern terminus of the *Erie Canal*, but the project was abandoned. The inhabitants are largely engaged in ship-building and brick-making. A branch of the *New York Central Railway* connects Athens with Schenectady, and has added much to its prosperity. Above Athens and Hudson, on the east side of the river, is *Rogers Island*, behind which the shipping of New York merchants was concealed during the Revolutionary War. At that time the island was densely wooded, and formed an effectual screen.

The ill-fated steamer *Swallow* was lost just off Athens.

COLUMBIAVILLE.

Stockport, Columbia County, N. Y.
119 *miles from New York.*

On the west side of the river is a promontory, with a light-house tower, which old river pilots call "*Chancy Tinker*," but which is now known as *Four-mile Point.*

Directly opposite to this is the mouth of Columbiaville Creek, on which, a short distance from the river, are large flannel mills.

COXSACKIE.

Coxsackie, Greene County, N. Y.
123 *miles from New York.*

This village is on the west side of the river. Its name is derived from an Indian word signifying "cut banks." The chief occupations of the inhabitants are ship-building, farming, and fishing. The headland nearly opposite is *Newtown Hook*. A mile below Coxsackie are the extensive vineyards of Mr. Ezra Fitch.

STUYVESANT.

Stuyvesant, Columbia County, N. Y.
125 miles from New York.

Formerly *Kinderhook Landing*. The village of Kinderhook is 4 miles inland. Ex-President *Martin Van Buren* lived there for many years before his death.

NEW BALTIMORE.

New Baltimore, Albany County, N. Y.
127 miles from New York.

The chief business of this place is ship-building. There are several yards with complete sets of ways, etc. Schooners, sloops, and barges are the craft which are built.

SCHODAC.

Schodac, Rensselaer County, N. Y.
132 miles from New York.

A small village on the east bank of the river. Good farming lands lie along the river, and the surrounding region is a pleasant rolling country. The name is of Indian rigin, signifying "a meadow."

COEYMAN'S.

Coeyman's, Albany County, N. Y.
132 miles from New York.

This village is on the west bank of the river. Its name (pronounced *Quy-mans*) is that of one of its early settlers. The range of mountains seen to the westward are the *Helderbergs*.

A little below Coeyman's, near the west shore, is a high rocky island on which the boundaries of four counties meet, namely, Albany, Greene, Columbia, and Rensselaer. This island was named by the Dutch *Beeren*, or *Bear Island*; and on its summit once stood the "Castle" of *Rensselaerstein*, from whose wall Nicholas Koorn, the agent of Killian Van Rensselaer, the Patroon, compelled passing vessels to dip their colors and pay tribute, or take the chances of being sunk by the ordnance of the fort. An amusing account of the whole difficulty between Governor Kieft of New Amsterdam, and the Patroon, is given in "Knickerbocker's" History of New York.

CASTLETON.

Schodac, Rensselaer Co., N. Y.
135 miles from New York.

A small and compact village, built upon a steep hillside on the eastern bank of the river. The domes and spires of Albany, 9 miles distant, may be seen from this point.

Castleton Bar, formerly known as the *Overslaugh*, has always been a serious impediment to navigation at this point. As early as 1790,

State appropriations were made for the purpose of improving the channel, but all efforts were unavailing until the present system of dykes was commenced. A. Van Santvoord, Esq., of Albany, President of the Day Line of New York and Albany Steamers, and other prominent citizens of Albany and Troy, had the subject brought before the State Legislature, and work was begun in 1863. In 1868 the U. S. Government assumed the work of completing the dykes, and they may now be seen stretching for several miles along the river, effectually accomplishing the purpose for which they were intended.

GREENBUSH,
Greenbush, Rensselaer Co., N. Y.,
144 *miles from New York,*

Is situated on the east side of the river opposite to Albany. Its population is largely made up of employés on the great railway lines which meet here from all parts of the Eastern States and from New York.

Along the river bank, both above and below the village proper, as handsome houses, and many pleasant-looking villas and cottages may be seen on the high bluff which rises beyond the alluvial flats that border the river.

Greenbush is a translation of the old Dutch name, which was doubtless appropriate in its day. During the French War in 1755, Greenbush was a military rendezvous, and again in 1812 the United States Government established extensive barracks whence troops were forwarded to the Canadian frontier.

STANWIX HALL,
Albany, N. Y.,

(Corner of Broadway and Maiden Lane.)

Adjoining New York Central & Hudson River and Rensselaer & Saratoga Railroad Depots.

First-Class in Every Respect.

TERMS, $3.00 PER DAY.

Delavan Peck,   Proprietor.

ALBANY.

Albany County, N. Y.
144 *miles from New York.*

HOTELS—*Delavan, Stanwix, Congress Hall, and City Hotel.*

THIS city lies upon the west bank of the Hudson River, near the middle of the county, and embraces a strip of land about one mile wide, extending thirteen and a half miles in a northwest direction, to the northern boundary of the county. Before incorporation it was known under the names of "Beverwyck," "William Stadt," and "New Orange." The seat of the State Government, originally fixed at New York City, was removed to this place in 1798. The early growth of the city was exceedingly slow; its population numbering less than 10,000 at the end of a century from its incorporation, which was in 1686. In 1714, when a century old, it contained only 3,329 inhabitants, nearly 500 of whom were slaves. Steam navigation, originated by Fulton on the Hudson in 1807, and the completion of the Erie Canal in 1825, each gave powerful impulses to its growth, and in less than half a century it added more than 50,000 to its population. In 1865, the census report shows about 63,000. The whole city, comprised within the limits of Pearl, Steuben, and Beaver Streets, in 1676, was surrounded by wooden walls, with openings for musketry. There were six gates to the city, and the maintenance of these fragile defences was the source of unceasing contention between the authorities and the inhabitants. A portion of these walls were remaining so late as 1812; they were thirteen feet in height, and made of timber about a foot square. The city has many handsome avenues, and the walks and drives about the city are exceedingly beautiful. A walk of half a mile from the city brings to view the verdure-clad mountains of Vermont and the towering Catskills. The first railroad in the State of New York, and the second in the United States, was opened from Albany to Schenectady in 1831. The commerce of Albany is very considerable.

COMMUNICATIONS.

Besides the great natural means of communication which the river affords, the city is connected with New York by two lines of railroad, the *Hudson River* and the *Harlem*. The *New York Central Railroad* and the *Erie Canal* connect it with the Great Lakes. Through Troy it communicates with Northern New York, Vermont, and Canada by the *Rensselaer & Saratoga* and *Troy & Boston* railways, and by the Champlain Canal. By the *Boston & Albany Railway*, it communicates with the New England States, and by the *Albany & Susquehanna Railway* with Binghamton and the coal regions of Pennsylvania.

TRADE AND MANUFACTURES.

The manufactures are extensive and varied. Its numerous *stove foundries* and *breweries* are on an immense scale. Seventy thousand barrels of ale are made annually at one brewery. The *workshops* of the Central Railroad give employment to more than one thousand persons. Its other manufactures are varied and extensive. The sales of barley amount to more than 2,000,000 bushels per annum, most of which is consumed by the brewers. *Lumber* is another very important article of trade. Albany is also one of the leading *cattle-marts* of the country. The markets at Bull's Head in New York, and at Brighton, near Boston, receive a large portion of their supplies from here.

PUBLIC BUILDINGS.

The *State buildings* include the Capitol, State Hall, State Library, Geological and Agricultural Hall, Normal School, and State Arsenal and Armory. The *City Hall* is an elegant structure, faced with Sing Sing marble, and surmounted by a gilded dome. The *Albany Exchange*, a massive granite building, is situated on Broadway, at the foot of State Street, and contains the Post-office.

INSTITUTIONS.

Besides Public Schools, the Educational Institutions are the *Albany Academy*, *Albany Female Academy*, *Albany Female Seminary*, *Albany Institute*, and the *Albany Industrial School*. The public schools afford instruction to 20,000 children of both sexes, and are conducted at an annual expense of $50,000. There are two *Christian Associations*, Protestant and Catholic, the former being the oldest institution of the kind in the United States. The *Dudley Observatory*, on an eminence in the northern border of the city, was incorporated

April 2, 1852; it was founded through the munificence of Mrs. Blandina Dudley, who gave $90,000 for its construction and endowment. The building, constructed in the form of a cross, is admirably arranged, and is furnished with some of the largest and finest instruments ever constructed. It has an extensive library attached. The *Albany Medical College* and the *Law School of the University of Albany* are on Eagle Street, and have all the facilities for teaching the respective sciences. The *Albany Almshouse, Insane Asylum*, and a *Fever Hospital* are located upon a farm of 116 acres, one and a half miles southwest of the city, and are under the management of the city authorities. The *Industrial School* building is located on the same farm. The *Albany City Hospital*, on Eagle Street, was incorporated in 1849. The *Albany Orphan Asylum*, on Washington Street, at the junction of the Western Turnpike, was incorporated in 1831; it was erected, as was the City Hospital, by private subscription; it is now aided by State funds. The *St. Vincent Orphan Asylum*, incorporated in 1849, is under the charge of the Sisters of Mercy. The male department, two miles west of the Capitol, is under the charge of the Christian Brothers.

CHURCHES.

The first church (Ref. Prot. D.) was formed in 1640. A Lutheran Church existed in 1680. The first Protestant Episcopal Church (St. Peter's) was erected in 1715; it stood in the centre of State Street, opposite Chapel Street. The communion plate of this church was presented to the Onondagas by Queen Anne. The most costly edifices are the Catholic Cathedral of the Immaculate Conception, corner of Eagle and Lydius Streets, and the St. Joseph's (R. C.) Church. In 1858 there were forty-eight churches in the city.

Water is supplied to the city from Rensselaer Lake, about five miles west of the City Hall, and 225 feet above the level of the water of the Hudson. This lake covers thirty-nine acres, and its capacity is 180,000,000 gallons. A brick conduit conveys the water to Bleecker Reservoir, on Patroon Street, whence it is distributed through the city. This reservoir has a capacity of 30,000,000 gallons. The cost of the construction of these works was upwards of $1,000,000.

An important event in the recent history of Albany was the construction of the railroad bridge over the Hudson. It was completed in March, 1866. The total length of this bridge is now 4,009 feet, or over three-fourths of a mile. The approaches consist of embankments and masonry, leaving the bridge proper 2,016 feet in length. It has twenty spans—three over the Albany basin, each 66 feet in length; six across the river, two of which form the draw, 112 feet each, and the other four fixed spans, 172 feet each. The remaining eleven extend across the flats, and are 66 feet each, except one of 71 feet. Its height is 30 feet above ordinary summer tide level. Piers are of cut stone, quarried at Amsterdam and Tribe's Hill, on the line of the New York Central Railway, and from Kingston, on the Hudson River, in Ulster County. The superstructure is of iron, sufficiently wide for two tracks. Its cost has been $1,150,000.

SARATOGA SPRINGS, N. Y.

JAMES H. WRIGHT,
LEADING TAILOR & CLOTHIER,
117 & 119 BROADWAY,

A few doors south of the United States Hotel.

A large assortment of the Finest Goods. Artistic Cutters. Prices moderate. Suits to order at one day's notice. Established 1855.

A full line of Gentlemen's Furnishing Goods of every description at popular prices.

CHAPTER III.

THE HOTELS.

The hotels at Saratoga Springs are among the largest, the most costly, elegant, and comfortable in the world. For nearly a century people have journeyed to these springs, to drink their healing waters; and, as one day's visit is hardly worth the while they have sought a home here during the summer season. It is this that has caused the village to open its doors so freely, and to build up, from a small beginning, a system of hotels and boarding-houses unlike anything else to be found. Added to this came, in time, the demands of the merely pleasure-seeking, fashionable world. People came to the springs for the sake of the gay company gathered here, and from year to year the hotels have grown, expanding their wings and adding room beyond room, till they cover acres of ground, and the halls and piazzas stretch out into miles. They have a bewildering fashion here of repeating the wondrous tale of these things. They talk about the miles of carpeting; the thousands upon thousands of doors and windows; the hundreds of miles of telegraph wires; vast acres of marble floors; and tons of eatables stored in the pantries, till one is lost in admirable confusion. It is all true and that is the wonder of it.

As for the management that governs it all, it is more remarkable than the gilding and mirrors. It is a sort of high science, unequaled in the world, combining in a delightful mixture, the "ease of mine inn," such as the English essayist never knew, and a perfection of detail and freedom from friction that is as pleasant as it is wonderful. Ask for anything you like in the known world, and, if it can be found, it will be provided.

Saratoga's face is her fortune, and it is said that the entire town devotes its days and nights to the comfort of the tourist. Of course, if this is true, and it undoubtedly is, the tourist should be indeed happy. If he is not, it is safe to say it is his own fault. In speaking of these hotels, the four great houses are mentioned first, because they are the largest. The smaller ones stand in the immediate neighborhood of these greater houses, and will be noticed in the order of their size. The numerous boarding houses will be considered in the next chapter.

Congress Hall

Is built on the site of the old and famous hotel of the same name which was burned in 1866, and occupies the larger part of the square bounded by Broadway, East Congress, Spring and Putnam Streets. Its situation is in the very centre of the gay and fashionable hotel world of Saratoga, and is admirably arranged for seeing all the attractive phases of the "great watering-place" life. Its frontage on Broadway, the principal street of the town, is 416 feet, with a high promenade piazza 20 feet wide and 249 feet in length, commanding a view of the most brilliant portion of Saratoga. From the Broadway front two immense wings, 300 feet long, extend to Putnam Street, the northern wing, running along Spring Street and overlooking the celebrated Hathorn and Hamilton Springs on one side, and with the central wing which runs parallel with it, enclosing a very beautiful garden-plot. The southern front commands a full view of the famous Congress and Columbian Springs, and the beautiful Congress Park, which has been very artistically arranged and adorned this season, at great expense, by the Congress and Empire Spring Co. Ample piazzas extend around the back of the hotel, overlooking the grass and garden-plots of the interior court, affording cool and shady retreats in the afternoon, when the most entrancing music is discoursed by the celebrated Bernstein Orchestra of New York.

Congress Hall is built in the most substantial manner of brick, with brown-stone trimmings, and presents one of the most graceful architectural appearances in Saratoga. Its walls are 20 inches thick and hollow in the centre, thus securing great strength and protection from heat of summer. The roof is a Mansard, with three pavilions, which afford wide and delightful views from the

CONGRESS HALL, Saratoga Springs, N. Y. Hathorn & Cook, Proprietors.
Opens June 1st.
HATHORN SPRING, 75 FEET NORTH; CONGRESS SPRING, 20 FEET SOUTH;
COLUMBIAN SPRING, 200 FEET SOUTH; HAMILTON SPRING, 75 FEET EAST.

promenades on top. Interior fire-walls are provided to prevent the spread of fire, and Otis elevators afford easy access to all the floors of the house. The rooms are all large, high and well ventilated, and properly provided with annunciators, gas, etc. The halls, dining-rooms, parlors, and offices are of grand proportions, and are furnished and finished with a quiet elegance that is an assurance of comfort and neatness in all its departments, and comports with the taste of its patrons. During the spring of 1876 extensive repairs have been made, among which are a material improvement in the *ventilation* of the dining-room and kitchen, and the introduction *of Steam Heating Apparatus* on the main floor for use whenever changes in the temperature require it. *Hot and cold water* have been carried to every floor, and a large number of baths and closets added for the convenience of guests.

There has also been a complete renovation of the furniture, and the rooms, halls, and parlors have been recarpeted, and the walls refinished; and the furnishing of the public parlors, reception rooms, office, and dining-room completely renewed. The laundry has been greatly improved and its facilities increased, and the entire hotel materially improved in all its interior arrangements.

The rooms of Congress Hall are all larger, and therefore afford pleasanter and more healthy apartments than any other hotel in Saratoga, and will accommodate over 1,000 guests in the most comfortable style. The beds are the easiest and best spring and hair mattresses to be found in this country, and ample presses, closets, etc. afford all desirable conveniences. The ball-room of the Congress is one of the finest in northern New York, being most exquisitely frescoed and adorned with costly chandeliers and ornaments. It is in the block across Spring street, but is connected with the north wing of the hotel by a light, graceful iron bridge suspended over the street, properly covered and protected, which, when illuminated on hop nights, is very picturesque.

Congress Hall is favored with a superior class of visitors, which annually include some of the finest families of our metropolitan cities, whose names are at once recognized in the most refined society; and it is the intention of the present proprietors, Messrs. Hathorn and Cooke, to maintain for the Congress the excellent reputation which it has enjoyed for so many years.

THE GRAND UNION HOTEL,
SARATOGA SPRINGS.
The Largest and most Magnificent in all its appointments of any in the World.

The Grand Union.

This palatial hotel occupies almost the entire square bounded by Broadway, Congress, Federal and Washington streets, in the very center of the town. It is a magnificent structure of brick and iron of modern style, with a street frontage of 2,400 feet. It is undoubtedly the largest and most elegantly furnished watering-place hotel in the world. Along its entire Broadway front of 800 feet runs a graceful iron piazza three stories high, affording a splendid promenade which overlooks the liveliest portion of Broadway, and the beautiful Congress Park and Spring. The interior arrangements of this hotel are unsurpassed for completeness, convenience and elegance by any watering-place hotel in the world. The main entrance and office is at the center of the Broadway front, in the rotunda, eighty feet in diameter, which extends to the top of the house, with balconies on each of the five stories overlooking the entrance and grand saloon about the office. To the left of the office are reception rooms and the grand saloon parlor, the most beautifully decorated and handsomely furnished drawing-room in the world, and in the summer evenings, during the season, presents the most brilliant scene of watering-place festivities to be found.

Passing through the drawing-room we find other smaller private parlors, and turning to the right into the Congress street wing we enter the spacious and elegant dining-hall, 60 feet wide, 275 feet long, very high, beautifully frescoed, and furnished with splendid mirrors, which reflect the festal scene, and add new lustre to the brilliant assemblies which congregate, during the season, in this sumptuous dining-hall.

During the Spring of 1876 the dining-room was lengthened 75 feet, a new fire-proof kitchen and serving-rooms added, and the ventilation of the whole cuisine department made the most perfect possible. The dining-hall and its appurtenances are now undoubtedly the finest and most complete in the world.

The rooms of the hotel are furnished in elegant style, and many are arranged in suites for family use, handsomely frescoed, and supplied with pure, fresh, running spring water, hot and cold, in every room. This important improvement has been made during the past Spring, and a serious inconvenience heretofore experienced has been remedied. Three elevators are now in operation, and guests are conveyed to and from the five floors with the utmost ease and dispatch. The hotel fronts on three streets, thus affording a large number of outside rooms, while the rear rooms open upon the handsome interior court-square, beautifully adorned with trees, shrubs and flowers, presenting a delightful view of genuine artistic landscape gardening. On three sides of this interior court is a wide promenade piazza, which affords delightful retreat, and yet commands a scene of entrancing beauty.

The new ball-room, 60 x 85 feet, built in 1876, is most beautifully proportioned and frescoed, and adorned with balconies of the most attractive character. Yvon's Grand Centennial Picture, "The Genius of America," painted expressly for the late Mr. Stewart, occupies one entire end of the room.

The assemblies in this beautiful hall are unexcelled in brilliancy by any similar entertainments in the country. Gilmore's world-renowned band of 25 performers supplies the music, and concerts are given every morning on the piazzas of the hotel, and hops every evening in the ball-room.

For the entertainment of the children a "Matinée Dansante," under the direction of Prof. Manuel, is given every Wednesday afternoon. Garden Parties and summer-night "Fête Champêtres" will be given frequently during the season, and a "German" once each week. No effort or expense is spared by the managers to secure the highest enjoyment possible to the guests of the Grand Union at these entertainments.

Billiard tables and new bowling alleys are provided for the exclusive use of guests, and all facilities that can conduce to comfort and entertainment are provided by the liberal management of this palatial hotel.

Its past management has secured for it a most enviable reputation, but the plans which the late Mr. Stewart had devised for the further convenience and enjoyment of the guests, surpassing the liberality of past years, are being completed and will be fully carried out, thus winning for the Grand Union the pre-eminence for completeness, vastness and elegance, of all the watering-place hotels in the world.

The United States Hotel.

This magnificent structure was completed in June, 1874, and is situated on the block bounded by Broadway and Division Street, on the site of the old United States Hotel, around which so many pleasant memories cluster, but which was burned a few years ago. It constitutes one continuous line of buildings, six stories high, over 1,400 feet in length, containing 917 rooms for guests, and is the largest hotel in the world. The architectural appearance is exceedingly elegant and beautiful. It is Norman in style, and its Mansard roof is embellished with pediments, gables, dormer windows and cuestings, and three large pavilions.

The building covers and encloses seven acres of ground in the form of an irregular pentagon, having a frontage of 232 feet on Broadway, 656 feet on Division Street, with "Cottage Wing" on the south side of the plaza, extending west from the main front for 566 feet. This wing is one of the most desirable features of this admirably-arranged house, as it affords families and other parties, the same quiet and seclusion which a private cottage would afford, together with the attention and conveniences of a first-class hotel. The rooms of this wing are arranged in suites of one to seven bedrooms, with parlor, bath-room, and water-closet in each suite. Private table is afforded if desired, and the seclusion and freedom of a private villa may be enjoyed here, to be varied, at will, by the gayer life of the hotel and watering place.

The main front and entrance is on Broadway, in which is the elegant drawing-room, superbly furnished with Axminster carpets, carved walnut and marble furniture, frescoed ceilings, elegant lace curtains, and costly chandeliers and mirrors. The room is rich and tasteful in its entire arrangements. Across the hall is the ladies' parlor, furnished with exquisite taste; and beyond, at the corner of the Broadway and Division Street fronts, are the gentlemen's reading-rooms and the business offices of the hotel. To the west of the office in the Division Street wing, is the dining-hall, 52 by 212 feet with 20½ feet ceiling; beyond which are the private drawing-rooms, the children's ordinary, carving-rooms, etc. The grand ball-room, 112 by 53 feet, with ceilings 26 feet high, is on the second floor of the Division Street wing, and is decorated with artistic and appropriate adornments.

The arrangement of the sleeping apartments of this hotel is excellent, and its rooms are furnished with gas, water, and marble basins throughout. It is the only hotel in Saratoga that is thoroughly plumbed and has running water in all its rooms. All the rooms are connected with the office by an electric annunciator. The entire building is divided into five sections by thick, fire-proof walls, and the openings through them are protected by heavy iron doors, thus affording great protection in case of fire. There are also fire-hydrants in each section, with hose attached, on each floor. Two elevators, of Otis Brothers' manufacture, are used solely for conveying guests to the various floors of the house, and every convenience that modern ingenuity has devised has been adopted in equipping this elegant hotel for its immense summer business. Upon the Broadway front is a fine piazza, 233 feet long, three stories high, overlooking the center of the village; and one on Division Street, 200 feet in length. Extensive piazzas, 2,900 feet in length, for promenades, encircle the large interior court, which is ornamented with beautiful shade-trees, sparkling fountains, graceful lawn-statuary, and meandering walks; and, during the evening, when illuminated with colored lights and lanterns, and enlivened with exquisite music, the scene is brilliant and fascinating in the extreme.

In fact, everything that is needed to make the hotel attractive and convenient is found here, and the United States Hotel stands unexcelled in its furnishing and arrangements by any of the hotels of the great watering-place. As one looks upon this palatial structure, and carefully inspects the detailed arrangements for the perfect convenience and comfort of its guests, he can but be amazed at the enterprise and courage of its owners, who have opened to the world this stupendous establishment. This immense and elegant hotel is managed by gentlemen of great experience. The Hon. James M. Marvin, who is well known to all old frequenters of Saratoga, has the general control of the whole interest, while Messrs. Tompkins, Perry, Gage, and Jonvrin have the supervision of the interior arrangements of the house. Their experience in our metropolitan hotels specially fits them for this important department, and guests can rely upon having everything provided that will conduce to their comfort and happiness.

The Clarendon Hotel.

This excellent house stands on Broadway, a short distance south of Congress Street, on one of the pleasantest sites in the village. The Clarendon is the only hotel in Saratoga which is painted white, with green blinds, presenting that clean, neat appearance which distinguishes so many New England villages, and produces a truly rural effect among the beautiful shade-trees that surround it. It pleasantly contrasts with the more metropolitan architecture and colors which obtain among the other hotels. It partly incloses within its wings a depression or valley, ornamented with shade trees, among which stands the tasteful pagoda covering the popular Washington Spring. The Leland Spring, named in honor of the affable proprietor of the hotel, is also within these grounds. These spring waters are among the most valuable of the Saratoga waters, the Washington Spring being a tonic water, highly prized by Saratoga residents, and popular with the visitors. Congress Grove is immediately opposite the Clarendon, and such of its guests as prefer Congress or Columbian waters to that which springs within their own dooryard can easily reach them. This hotel is largely patronized by a class of visitors who do not desire to mingle with the somewhat promiscuous company which fills the larger hotels. The Clarendon can accommodate about 500 guests, and its arrangement is every way calculated to give satisfaction to those who patronize it as a summer resort. An excellent band discourses delightful music daily, morning and evening, from the piazza overlooking the interior court, which is illuminated in the evening, and presents a very picturesque effect.

The Clarendon is owned by Mr. Charles E. Leland, a younger member of the Leland family whose name has become so celebrated in connection with first-class hotels in America. He is also proprietor of the famous Delavan House in Albany, N. Y., which has become so famous under his care as a superb hotel, and the new and elegant Rossmore Hotel at Broadway, Forty-second Street and Seventh Avenue, New York. The Rossmore is one of the most costly and magnificent hotels in America. It is built in the most modern style of hotels, with every convenience that human genius could devise, and furnished with a luxuriance and elegance unsurpassed by any hotel in the world. With three such

CLARENDON HOTEL, Saratoga Springs, N. Y. Charles E. Leland, *Proprietor*. Also Proprietor of the famous *Delavan Hotel* of Albany and the new and elegant *Rossmore Hotel*, Broadway, 41st Street and Seventh Avenue, New York City. Price, $4.00 per day.

elegant hotels under his control, Mr. Leland needs no further testimony as to his ability to supply all the wants and please the taste of the refined and aristocratic patrons of his famous hotels.

The Columbian Hotel.

Mr. D. A. Dodge, proprietor, is a new hotel on Broadway, opposite Congress Park, and just south of Crystal Spring. A more beautiful and central location is not to be found in the limits of the famous watering-place. It is just where everybody wants to be, and yet is free from noise, is homelike, and patronized by superior society. To those who visit Saratoga for genuine recreation, for sight-seeing, or for health, the Columbian Hotel offers special advantages. Congress, Columbian, Crystal, and Washington Springs are in full view from the piazzas, and the popular drives to the Geyser Spring region and Ballston Springs are past this hotel. The house is built of brick, in a very substantial manner, and has been materially enlarged during the spring of 1876, so that it has now a frontage of 121 feet on Broadway, with a wide two story piazza 115 feet long, overlooking Congress Park and the fashionable drive of the town. The back piazza, overlooking its own beautiful grounds and those of the Clarendon Hotel, including Washington Spring, is also 115 feet in length, and as one of these piazzas is always shaded, a pleasant retreat is furnished at any hour of the day. All the rooms of the Columbian have pleasant and open outlooks, and are richly furnished with black walnut and upholstered furniture. Everything about it is well arranged and delightful, and it is kept with a neatness and quiet order that insures comfort and real enjoyment. With its charming location, its perfect neatness, and its agreeable society, what more could be asked? Besides, its prices are very reasonable. It will accommodate from 250 to 300 guests.

The Holden House

Is situated on one of the pleasantest portions of Broadway, just north of the Marvin House. The building is of brick, and has a pleasant veranda on its front, commanding a fine view of the principal street of the village. It was opened in 1871, and proved to be one of the most popular of the smaller hotels.

COLUMBIAN HOTEL,
Broadway, opposite Congress Park, Saratoga Springs, N. Y.
D. A. DODGE, PROPRIETOR.

The Windsor Hotel.

This new and elegant house was built in the Spring of 1876, and opened for the first time to the public in June. It stands on the corner of Broadway and William street, on higher ground than any other hotel in Saratoga, and commands a magnificent view of the beautiful Congress Park, Broadway, and the great hotels of the town. The house is constructed in the most modern style of arrangement, and its rooms are supplied with all the conveniences, such as closets, passenger elevator, etc., which go to make a real first-class hotel. The ceilings are high, the rooms large and well ventilated, with a very pleasant outlook from each, while the prospect from its upper stories is beautiful. From the roof of the house the view commands a wide range of country, embracing in its scope several villages in Saratoga county, the Hudson Valley, the Green Mountains in the distant East, and the Greenfield Hills and Adirondack Mountains on the west, with the whole of the village of Saratoga Springs and Congress Park in immediate prospect. On two sides of the house is a wide piazza, three stories high, which commands the most delightful view of any hotel piazza in Saratoga.

The house is so situated that it overlooks the entire length of Broadway, the principal street of the village, and the broad, handsomely shaded avenue, with its bustle and gorgeous pageant, and mammoth hotels on either side, forms a vista remarkably charming, and unequaled in the great watering-place. The interior arrangements of the house are in keeping with its handsome surroundings—the furniture rich, and the grand saloon parlor elegantly furnished and decorated. The cuisine department is superintended by most competent caterers, and it is the intention of the proprietor, Mr. Poole, to keep a house inferior to none in this famous watering-place. The popular drive to Geyser Spring and the other Spouting Springs is through Broadway in front of the Windsor. The most important springs are but a few rods from the hotel, and all the principal attractions of the village are close by.

The appearance of the house, its beautiful situation, its new and fresh condition, its modern conveniences, its experienced management, and its fair prices, combine to make the Windsor a very desirable place of resort for the summer.

WINSOR HOTEL, SARATOGA SPRINGS.

The Marvin House

Is situated on the corner of Broadway and Division Street, directly opposite the new United States Hotel. It is one of the best constructed hotels in Saratoga, and will accommodate about 300 guests. The building is of brick, and is of modern and improved arrangement in its interior plan, having been built but a few years. It is five stories high, surmounted with a Mansard roof, and presents a very neat and attractive exterior on the fashionable avenue of the town. The house fronts two of the most prominent streets of the town, and its rooms are particularly desirable, as they command views of the liveliest portions of Broadway and the business center of the place. Extending along the Broadway front is a fine broad piazza two stories high, which

commands the most extended view of Broadway of any piazza in Saratoga, overlooking it from Congress Park and Spring for a distance north of over half a mile; thus affording a delightful lounging-place on a summer's day, and an excellent resort for sight-seeing. During the spring of 1874 the office was remodeled and very much improved, so that the Marvin has now one of the pleasantest offices and reading-rooms of all the Saratoga hotels. The Marvin is but a few steps from the Railroad Depot, and free carriages and trusty porters await the arrival of all trains. The hotel is kept open throughout the year.

The Waverly House

Is situated in the upper part of Saratoga, on Broadway, in a beautiful and quiet portion of the village, and yet easily accessible to the gayety and fashion of the large hotels. This is the nearest hotel to the celebrated High Rock, Saratoga Star, Empire, Excelsior, and Seltzer Springs, and within a few minutes' walk of the Congress, Washington, Hathorn, and Crystal Springs.

It stands on higher ground than any other hotel in Saratoga, and is kept with a view to affording the greatest comfort and luxuries to its guests. Its patrons are among the finest classes that visit Saratoga. Parties and families wishing rooms and board for the season will find reasonable terms and the most polite attention.

The American

Forms another of the group of hotels in the immediate vicinity of Congress and Hathorn Springs. It is at the corner of Broadway and Washington Street, and is kept open all the year.

DRS. STRONG'S REMEDIAL INSTITUTE.

This excellent institution is situated on Circular street, the most beautiful avenue in Saratoga, only a short distance from the great hotels, and one block from the Congress Park.

The institute was established several years ago, and has enjoyed a superior reputation for its treatment of invalids, as well as for its hotel and boarding accommodations, and will accommodate 200 guests. Being somewhat removed from the bustle and confusion of the large hotels, it affords a delightful retreat for persons of impaired health; while refined and cultivated people will find its society more congenial than that of the more public houses. Among its annual patrons are Rev. Theodore L. Cuyler, D.D.; Ex-Gov. Wells, of Va.; Mr. Robert Carter, of the firm of Carter Brothers, publishers, of New York, and many others of like position in society. The institution is supplied with new and the most improved appliances now known to medical science, among which are the Electro-thermal, Sulphur Air, Turkish, and Russian Baths, Swedish Movement Cure, the Equalizer or Vacuum Treatment, Oxygen Inhalations, Gymnastics, and other varieties of Hydropathy and Medicine. The whole institution, with its treatment, is supervised by Drs. Sylvester S. and Sylvester E. Strong, regular physicians, graduated at the Medical Department of the University of New York.

The elegance and convenience of the Bath Department is unsurpassed in this country, or the world. The buildings are heated by steam, so that the temperature throughout the house is moderated to a healthful uniformity, and in winter is brought to the condition of a summer climate. Circulars giving a full description of the institution, its remedial agents and rare appliances, its remarkable success in the treatment of *Nervous, Lung, Female,* and *Chronic Diseases,* with distinguished references, terms, etc., will be furnished by the proprietors on application.

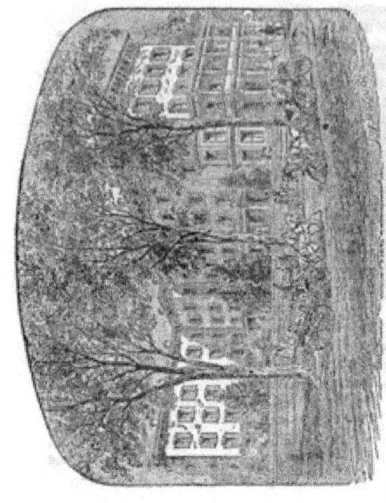

DRS. STRONG'S REMEDIAL INSTITUTE, SARATOGA SPRINGS, N. Y.,

For the cure of Nervous, Lung, Female, and Chronic Diseases, has Turkish, Russian, Roman, Sulphur, Air, Electro-thermal and Electro-thermal Baths, Vacuum Treatment, Movement Cure, Talahassi and Galvanic Electricity, with other new and efficient Remedial Agencies. For description of appliances, diseases and their successful treatment, terms, etc., send for circular. Endorsed by Rev. T. L. Cuyler, D.D.; Prof. Taylor Lewis, LL.D.; Bishop E. S. Janes, D.D., and others.

Dr. Robert Hamilton's Medical Institute.

On Franklin Street, is an institution for the treatment of various chronic and special diseases, and is conducted by one of Saratoga's most eminent physicians, who has long enjoyed a good reputation as a practitioner, and is a conscientious Christian gentleman. Many are familiar with his institution that stood on the corner of Broadway and Congress Street for many years, but was burned in the disastrous fire that swept away the Park Place and Crescent hotels.

In the spring of 1874, Dr. Hamilton removed to Franklin Street, one of the most quiet and beautiful streets in town, and has now one of the best institutions for the treatment of the various diseases "that flesh is heir to." He is one of the most reliable consulting physicians in Saratoga County, and, having long resided and practiced in Saratoga, and observed the effects of the various spring waters on different constitutions and in different diseases, is best qualified to give advice to those who wish to drink the mineral waters in a systematic way and to the best advantage. Dr. Hamilton makes a specialty of this practice, and is recognized as a most excellent authority on the subject.

The Institution is open as a summer boarding-house during the season, and is kept in good style, and in such a manner that no features of a medical institute are observable. The terms are very reasonable, and all the medical patrons will be most conscientiously and ably treated, and the pleasure-guests cared for with faithful attendance to their wants. We append a notice that appeared in the *Saratoga Sun*, April, 1874, which shows how Dr. Hamilton is regarded at home by those who know him best:

"Up to the time of the destruction of 'The Crescent' by fire there was probably no medical institute in Saratoga better known or so well known as the one kept by Dr. Robert Hamilton. His common-sense method of treatment, his thorough acquaintance with the medical properties of all the waters of all the springs, and the general tone of health, vigor, hopefulness, and social comfort which distinguished his practice made his institute popular with all his inmates, and famous throughout the land. Since the fire Dr. Hamilton has not, until this spring, been able to locate permanently, and his patients have been accommodated as best they could be in private boarding-houses. Now, however, he has taken the spacious and splendid buildings popularly known as 'The Summer Resort,' and will, the 1st of May, re-open there his medical institute, with ample and pleasant accommodations for a large number of patient and guests. 'The Summer Resort' is most conveniently located on Franklin Street, near all the springs, and in the most quiet, genteel, and accessible part of the village. Dr. Hamilton will soon take possession, and those who desire to avail themselves of the excellent methods of treatment and the superior advantages of his institut on will do wisely to make early application."

Send for circular of the Institute and terms for board to Dr. Robert Hamilton, Saratoga Springs, N. Y.

VAN NESS HOUSE, Burlington, Vt.
D. C. BARKER & CO., Proprietors.

The Van Ness House is a fine hotel, central in location, with a beautiful outlook upon Lake Champlain and the Adirondack Mountains. It is the largest hotel in Burlington, and will rank as one of the best hotels in New England.

MOUNT MANSFIELD HOTEL.

This celebrated place of Summer resort opens for visitors June 1st, with extra inducements to the public to visit it and its surroundings. Board will be at a reduced price, in harmony with the downward tendency of values. The proprietors are determined not to be excelled in their attention to guests, nor in courtesy to them by their employees.

The walks and drives cannot be surpassed. Sunset Hill, a short distance from the hotel, commands a fine view of the mountains and surrounding country. The drives are fine—Mount Mansfield, eight miles; Smuggler's Notch, one of the most wild and romantic places in the country, eight miles; Bingham's Falls, five miles; Moss Glen Falls, three and one half miles; Gold Brook, three miles; West Hill, two miles; Morrisville Falls, eight miles; Johnson's Falls, twelve miles; Nebraska, six miles. The Mount Mansfield is a new hotel, and has rooms for four hundred guests. The rooms are airy, large, and in suits or private parlors, as may be desired. The hotel is brilliantly lighted with gas made on the premises, and guests will therefore not be subject to any disagreeable smoke or smell from oil or camphene. Perfectly free from Hay Fever.

An extensive Livery is connected with the hotel, and abundant stable room for those who desire their own teams; also, Billiard-Tables, Bowling-Alleys, Café, Croquet Grounds, and Theatre; with Telegraph Office near the hotel. A carriage road has been constructed to the summit of Mount Mansfield (about five thousand feet high), on which is an excellent hotel, making the most delightful mountain trip possible. Fifty new rooms were added in the spring of 1875.

The route to Mount Mansfield Hotel is via the Vermont Central Railroad, leaving it at Waterbury station, Vt.; thence, a short distance by stage, to Stowe, through the finest scenery in the Green Mountains.

From the White Mountains, over the Portland and Ogdensburg Railroad, to Morrisville, Vt. Stages connect with the midday train.

N. P. KEELER, Manager,
STOWE, VT.

St. Lawrence Hall,

St. James St., Montreal.

F. GERIKEN, Proprietor,

Successor to H. HOGAN.

The above hotel, unrivaled for size and accommodation in the city, has, during the past winter, been entirely refurnished and renovated. From its central location, it is especially adapted for the convenience of tourists—all the principal places of interest being in close proximity. As an evidence of superiority, it has been patronized by the Government on all public occasions, and by H. R. H. the Prince of Wales, His Excellency the Governor General, His Imperial Highness the Grand Duke Alexis, &c.

The residence of the United States Consul is at this hotel.

The proprietor having purchased the interest of H. Hogan, would respectfully solicit a continuance of the favors extended to him for over twenty years.

J. T. BURKHOLDER, Manager.

OTTAWA HOTEL,

NOTRE DAME ST.   GREAT ST. JAMES ST.

MONTREAL, CANADA.

C. S. BROWNE & J. Q. PERLEY, Proprietors.

This Popular First-Class Hotel accommodates 400 Guests.

THE OTTAWA HOTEL covers the entire space of ground running between St. James and Notre Dame Streets, and has two beautiful fronts: the one on the right, in the above cut, represents the front on Notre Dame Street—the other on the left, the St. James Street front.

The House has been thoroughly REFITTED and FURNISHED, with every regard to comfort and luxury—has Hot and Cold Water, with Baths and Closets on each floor. The aim has been to make this the most

UNEXCEPTIONABLE FIRST-CLASS HOTEL IN MONTREAL.

The Manager respectfully informs the traveling public that he intends by constant attention to the wants of his patrons to make this hotel a comfortable home for travelers.

Carriages with attentive drivers, may be had at all times by application at the Office.

Coaches will also be found at the Railway Depot and Steamboat Landings, on the arrival of the several Trains and Steamers.

MONTREAL TELEGRAPH OFFICE IN THE HOUSE.

MONTREAL HOUSE,

CUSTOM HOUSE SQUARE,

MONTREAL.

DECKER & JUDD, - - - PROPRIETORS.

Is the neatest, coolest, best furnished, most pleasantly situated, and has more front rooms, for its size, than any hotel in the Dominion of Canada.

The hotel has a frontage of 180 feet on the Square and 120 on Commissioners Street, with an entrance on both, located on the high ground overlooking the harbor, and affording a most picturesque view of St. Helen's Island, the projected site of the Royal Albert Bridge, and the river for miles above and below the Victoria Bridge, affording to guests something of interest instead of huge stone and brick walls to look at. As it is situated within a block and a half of the great Cathedral de Notre Dame, and in close proximity to the New Post Office and principal Banks, etc., it is not only by far the most pleasantly, but as conveniently located as any hotel in the city.

The hotel is under the supervision of L. W. DECKER, who, now that he has sold out his interest in the "Albion," in which he did so successful a business for 20 years, will be able to give his undivided attention to the "Montreal House," where special effort will be made to make this house a favorite with tourists and pleasure seekers, and at the same time spare no pains to make it equally attractive to local custom and the general traveling public. It is kep in a manner quite up to any hotel in the city, and at prices not calculated to startle its guests.

ALBION HOTEL,

McGill and St. Paul Streets,

MONTREAL, CANADA.

Has for twenty years been the favorite resort of the traveling public of the United States, as well as of Canada, when visiting Montreal on business or pleasure. McGill Street is the great business thoroughfare of the City, and from its proximity to the principal houses of business, justly entitles THE ALBION to that large and increasing support it is receiving from the commercial class; while from its favorable position it commands a magnificent view of the River St. Lawrence, the Victoria Bridge, Victoria Square, and Mount Royal. It possesses every convenience which the traveling community can require, and we trust that our long experience in the business will give confidence to our friends that they will continue to enjoy at THE ALBION the advantage of a really first-class hotel at second-class prices.

DECKER, STEARNS & MURRAY

THE RECOLLET HOUSE,
MONTREAL.

BROWN & CLAGGETT,
Importers and Manufacturers of
Ladies' Dresses, Suits, Mantles, and Gents' Clothing,
THE DOMINION EMPORIUM FOR

Fine Shawls, Silks, Velvets, Laces, Ribbons, and Kid Gloves,
Ladies' and Gents' Furnishings,

AND

FANCY AND STAPLE DRY GOODS
Of every Description, Quality, and Style,

Cor. Notre Dame and St. Helen Sts.

N.B.—Our Cutter and Manager in the Dressmaking Department, was formerly in a leading house in New York.

PERRY'S

Parlor Boot and Shoe Store,

No. 375 Notre Dame Street,

MONTREAL,

IMPORTERS OF FRENCH AND AMERICAN FINE BOOTS
AND SHOES,

FOR LADIES, MISSES, AND CHILDREN ONLY.

A. PERRY Jr.

[LATE OF BURT'S, BROOKLYN]

P. S.—The proprietor (late with Burt's Fine Shoe House in NEW YORK and BROOKLYN) is well up in the wants of a Fine Shoe Business, and respectfully solicit a call.

This Store is one of the most comfortable establishments in Montreal.

American ladies will find such goods as will be found in **only one** place outside of Montreal, and that is PARIS !

LEXINGTON
CENTRAL STORAGE WAREHOUSE,

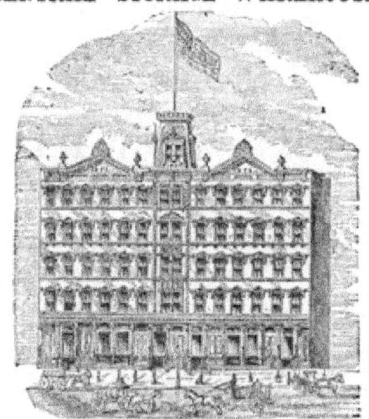

109, 111, 113 & 115 EAST 44th STREET, NEW YORK,
EAST OF THE GRAND CENTRAL DEPOT.

Large, elegant, very desirable and perfect Warehouses for the Storage and Safe-keeping of Furniture, Articles of Value, Works of Art, Baggage, Merchandise, &c., at the most reasonable rates.

The Warehouses, being in the immediate vicinity of "The Grand Central Depot," are convenient for parties out of town, and goods or baggage can be consigned direct to our Warehouses, or we will take charge of them at the depot on receiving letters of instruction, &c.

Goods, packages, &c., taken charge of at the Port of New York, and forwarded upon receipt of Bills of Lading, Invoices, Letters of Instruction, &c., to any place in this Country or Europe as directed. Charges for Freight, Insurance, &c., advanced. Warehouse receipts given on receipt of goods, and delivered to persons authorized to receive them.

A large Carriage Elevator conveys carriages and loaded trucks to upper floors of building without unloading. Watchmen at all times on the premises. Goods taken on Storage day or night. Ladies and Gentlemen are invited to call and examine our Warehouses before making arrangements for Storage elsewhere.

CORNELIUS O'REILLY & BROS., Proprietors and Owners of Buildings.

THE
HIGHLANDS OF THE HUDSON
BY DAYLIGHT.

THE STEAMER
MARY POWELL
LEAVES NEW YORK DAILY
(SUNDAYS EXCEPTED).

LEAVES GOING SOUTH.		LEAVES GOING NORTH.	
	A.M.	New York, from Vestry	P.M.
Rondout	5.30	St., Pier 39, at	3.30
Poughkeepsie	6.00	Cozzens'	6.00
Milton	6.45	West Point	6.10
New Hamburgh and Marlboro,	7.00	Cornwall	6.30
Newburgh	7.30	Newburgh	6.45
Cornwall	7.45	New Hamburgh and Marlboro,	7.15
West Point	8.05	Milton	7.30
Cozzens'	8.10	Poughkeepsie	7.45
Arrives in New York at 10.45		Arrives at Rondout	8.30

CONNECTS WITH EVENING TRAIN ON HUDSON RIVER R.R. AT POUGHKEEPSIE FOR THE NORTH.

Low Rate Excursion Tickets to Lake Mohunk via Wallkill Valley R.R., and Tickets to all points on Ulster and Delaware Railroad.

TROY HOUSE
TROY, N. Y.

This house has recently been REFITTED and REFURNISHED in the most thorough manner, making it

ONE OF THE FINEST HOTELS IN THE COUNTRY,

And greatly superior to any in the City of Troy.

I confidently assure my friends and the public that they will meet with every

COMFORT, LUXURY, AND DESIRABLE CONVENIENCE

At the Troy House, and will find the prices no higher than at any other first-class Hotel.

Gentlemen with their families, and others, will find the Troy House all that is desired.

Coaches will be in attendance to convey guests to and from the House.

J. W. STEARNS, Proprietor,
Late of Mansion House

BALLSTON SPA ARTESIAN LITHIA SPRING

The water of this remarkable Spring is shown by analysis to be twice as rich in valuable Remedial Agents as any other water found in Saratoga County, and to surpass in excellence all the Waters found in other parts of the United States. Flowing from a depth of six hundred and fifty feet, through a tube bored into the solid rock, it is not diluted or contaminated by surface water, as is generally the case with shallow springs.

Its medical properties partake of the most celebrated Springs of the world, and in fact combine the ingredients of all the principal ones in Europe and America. It is very strongly impregnated with that valuable mineral, *Lithia*, which is so effectual in dissolving the *Chalk*, or *Limestone* and *Urate* deposits in RHEUMATISM, GOUT, and GRAVEL, and has been successfully used by hundreds in these diseases, with quick and telling effect; as also in KIDNEY DISEASE, LIVER COMPLAINT, CATARRH, DYSPEPSIA, BILIOUSNESS, ACIDITY OF THE STOMACH, CONSTIPATION and PILES, and has proved itself a perfect panacea for these difficulties.

The large quantities of Lithia, Bromine, and Iodine which it contains, specially recommend it to the attention of every Physician.

ANALYSIS BY PROF. C. F. CHANDLER, Ph.D.

Chloride of Sodium	752.030 gr.	Sulphate of Potassa	0.030 gr.
Chloride of Potassium	33.976 "	Phosphate of Soda	0.050 "
Bromide of Sodium	3.643 "	Biborate of Soda	trace.
Iodide of Sodium	0.126 "	Alumina	0.077 "
Fluoride of Calcium	trace.	Silica	6.781 "
Bicarbonate of Lithia	7.750 "	Organic Matter	trace.
Bicarbonate of Soda	11.928 "		
Bicarbonate of Magnesia	120.622 "	Total per gal. (231 cub. in.)	1253.245
Bicarbonate of Lime	229.150 "		
Bicarbonate of Strontia	0.607 "	Carbonic Acid Gas	420.114 cub. in.
Bicarbonate of Baryta	3.881 "	Density	1.0159 "
Bicarbonate of Iron	1.581 "	Temperature	52 deg. F.

School of Mines, Columbia College, N. Y. April 22, 1868.

For the benefit of those who are not acquainted with the richness of the different Springs, we give a Statement of the quantity of mineral matter contained in one gallon of Water of the Springs which claims to be the most effective in disease :—

Ballston Artesian Lithia Spring	1253.245 gr.	Star Spring	618.695 gr.
Congress Spring	567.344 "	Seltzer Spring	401.680 "
Empire Spring	490.322 "	Excelsior	514.746 "
High Rock Spring	628.036 "	Gettysburgh Katalysine	266.936 "

The Water is carefully and securely bottled, and packed in boxes of four dozen Pints, and will bear transportation to any part of the world.

To prevent imposition, the corks are marked thus: **Artesian Spring Co., Ballston, N. Y.** Address

ARTESIAN LITHIA SPRING CO.,
Ballston Spa., N. Y.

ITHACA HOTEL.
ITHACA, N. Y.
A. SHERMAN & SON, Proprietors.

The above new Hotel was completed and opened for the reception of guests on the 30th of September, 1872.

It is centrally located for business, and convenient to CORNELL UNIVERSITY, THE GORGE, and other places of interest in and around Ithaca.

This house has been furnished throughout with new and costly furniture, and is provided with every modern improvement found in any FIRST-CLASS HOTEL in the country. Its rooms are large and airy, and great care has been taken in its construction to secure perfect ventilation. The table is constantly supplied with the luxuries of home and foreign markets, the assistants competent and attentive; and the proprietors pledge themselves that no pains or expense shall be spared to make the stay of the guests of the ITHACA HOTEL pleasant and agreeable.

LAKE CHAMPLAIN AND LAKE GEORGE

STEAMERS.

Pleasure Season of 1876.

LAKE CHAMPLAIN STEAMERS.

VERMONT, - - - - Capt. Rushlow.
ADIRONDACK, - - - Capt. Anderson.

Forming a daily line each way between Fort Ticonderoga and Plattsburgh, leaving Plattsburgh every morning at **7.30**, touching at all ports on the Lake, arriving at Fort Ticonderoga **12.00** noon. Leave Fort Ticonderoga **12.30** P.M., arriving at Plattsburgh **6.45** P.M.

Direct railroad connections at each end of the route.

LAKE GEORGE STEAMERS.

MINNEHAHA, - - - - Capt. Russell.
GANOUSKIE, - - - Capt. Hulett.

Leaving Caldwell every morning at **8** o'clock, making the usual landings, arrive at Baldwin Station **11.30** A.M., connecting direct with Lake Champlain Steamers as above.

Leave Baldwin Station **1.00** P.M., on arrival of train from Lake Champlain, arrives at Caldwell **5** P.M.

Through Tickets on sale at all Excursions Offices in New York, Philadelphia, Boston, &c., &c. Ask for Tickets via Lake Champlain and Lake George.

P. W. BARNEY, Supt.,
Burlington, Vt.

CLARENDON HOUSE,

CLARENDON SPRINGS, VT.

B. MURRAY & SONS, - - - - - Proprietors.

Open from middle of May to October.

TERMS:

Board, per Week,	$10.00 to $12.00
Children under Twelve, going to first table,	5.00 & 6.00
Servants,	5.00 & 6.00
Day Board,	2.50

☞ Carriages at West Rutland to meet all regular Railroad Trains. *Telegraph* communication, Livery and Boarding Stables connected with the House. Warm and Cold Baths. Cool nights, and no mosquitoes. Music, Billiards, Bowling, etc. Pleasant drives and *beautiful* scenery in every direction. References, if desired, in all principal cities.

Send for Pamphlet with description.

CLARENDON SPRINGS.

DISCOVERED IN THE HISTORIC YEAR 1776, ARE

Unequaled for Curing all Impurities of the Blood, Liver Complaint, Dyspepsia, Dropsy, and for Restoring Appetite and Physical Strength.

This water has no sediment, is delicious to drink, health-giving, and in bathing acts like a charm on the skin. Children come to us with pale faces and leave with ruddy cheeks.

ANALYSIS:

One gallon, or 235 inches of water contains :

Carbonic Acid Gas	46.16	cubic inch.
Nitrogen Gas	9.62	" "
Carbonate of Lime	3.02	grains.
Muriate of Lime, Sulphate of Soda, and Sulphate of Magnesia	2.74	"

One hundred cubic inches of the gas which was evolved from the water consist of—

Carbonic Acid Gas	0.05	cubic inch.
Oxygen Acid Gas	1.50	" "
Nitrogen Acid Gas	98.45	" "

Dr. AUGUSTUS A. HAYES, State Assayer for Massachusetts, says: "It is a remarkable water, containing nitrogen dissolved."

THE EQUINOX HOUSE
(FOOT OF MT. EQUINOX).

MANCHESTER, - - VERMONT.

Open from June to October.

ADDRESS, BY MAIL OR TELEGRAPH, **F. H. ORVIS.**

Manchester, the leading summer resort of the Green Mountains, is two hundred miles north of New York, fifty miles north of Troy, and thirty miles south of Rutland, on the Harlem Extension Division of the Central Vermont Railroad. It has about three miles of white marble sidewalks, finely shaded with elm and maple trees, and is the most charming summer resort in New England.

The trip to the top of Mt. Equinox should be taken by every visitor. An extended and magnificent view is obtained from the Summit House. The road is in fine order, and four-horse mountain wagons run to the top in two hours.

Manchester can be reached from New York during the summer in six and a half hours by Hudson River Railroad, via Troy. Drawing-Room Cars through without change.

Hudson River Night Steamers connect at Troy with 8:30 A.M. Train, reaching Manchester at 10:55 A.M.

New York Morning Papers reach Manchester 10:55 A.M.

Central Vermont Railroad Day Express brings Passengers from Montreal, Highgate Springs, St. Albans, Burlington, Stowe, &c., to Manchester direct. Drawing-Room Cars through.

From Saratoga, Trains going North connect at Rutland for Manchester; Trains going South connect at Troy for Manchester.

THE PUTNAM HOUSE,

PALATKA, - - FLORIDA.

Open from November to May.

ADDRESS, BY MAIL OR TELEGRAPH, **F. H. ORVIS.**

Palatka is situated on the west bank of the St. John's River, seventy miles south of Jacksonville. It is at the head of Navigation for ocean steamers, and at the mouth of the celebrated Ocklawaha River.

Hart's famous orange grove is immediately across the St. John's River, opposite the town.

Florida tourists should visit Palatka and make the trip up the romantic Ocklawaha to the wonderful Silver Spring.

Palatka can be reached by steamers daily from Jacksonville, and by the steamers Dictator and City Point from Charleston and Savannah, which run in connection with steamers from New York, and lines of Railroad from the North.

COZZENS' HOTEL.—*Cozzens' Landing, West Point, N. Y.*
GOODSELL BROTHERS, *Proprietors.*

This elegant and favorite summer resort stands on a commanding eminence on the west side of the Hudson, 230 feet above the river, and about one mile and a half south of the Military Academy of West Point. It commands one of the finest views on the Hudson, embracing the very heart of the Highlands, and the wildest and most picturesque scenery on this famous river. Its location is remarkably healthful; no cases of sickness having originated at this resort in twenty-five years. West Point was selected as the site of the Military Academy partly because of the healthfulness of the locality. Its location is particularly convenient for New York families, as it is but fifty miles distant, and gentlemen are enabled to visit New York daily, returning to Cozzens' at night if they desire. Among the many places of interest around Cozzens' are the U. S. Military Academy, where daily military exercises of interest occur, old Fort Putnam, Beverly Dock, Robinson House, Buttermilk Falls, etc. The drives among the historic Highlands are celebrated for their enchanting beauty, and one or two, including the five-mile drive to Crystal Lake, have recently been laid out. Distinguished visitors, including our national officials and celebrities, annually visit West Point Academy during the examinations, which begin on the 1st of June.

The hotel is built of brick, and is so constructed that all its rooms command delightful views of the river and mountain scenery. It will accommodate about 400 guests, who are the most refined and respected classes of our metropolitan society. The house is kept in a style to suit such patronage, and Cozzens' Hotel stands unrivaled among our summer resorts in its quiet elegance and comfort.

The table is not surpassed by any hotel in America in luxuries or style, and excellent music daily enlivens the enjoyments of this elegant and unexceptional resort. It can be reached by the Hudson River Railway to Garrison's Station, whence a steam-ferry conveys passengers to Cozzens' Dock; or by Day Line Steamers to West Point, with omnibus to Cozzens' Hotel, or the Mary Powell and Jas. W. Baldwin to Cozzens'. Carriages await at Cozzens' Dock and West Point the arrival of all boats and trains. Daily excursions may be made from New York, stopping for dinner and spending three or four hours at the hotel, returning to the city the same day. Passengers should not mistake the West Point or Government Hotel for Cozzens', but drive to *Cozzens' Hotel*, kept by *Goodsell Bros.*

THE
PALISADE MOUNTAIN HOUSE,

One of the finest summer hotels in the world, is situated on the Lydecker Point of the Palisades of the Hudson River, at Englewood, N. J., opposite Spuyten Duyvil. It is reached by Northern R. R. of N. J., of W. 23d St., or Chambers St., or Steamboats Adelphi and Alexis from foot of Harrison Street, New York. The situation is the most beautiful of any suburban hotel around New York City. The Palisades are four hundred feet or over above the level of the Ocean, and on one of their highest and most prominent outlooks stands the Mountain House. At its foot the Hudson washes the base of the cliffs on which it is built. To the north, bold sweeps of coast, marked with woody headlands and capped with a luxuriant forest, stretch away into the dim distance. Southerly, the spires of the city, the green hills of Staten Island, and the gleam of the Narrows fill the horizon; in front, a superb expanse of hill and dale, river, bay, and Sound spreads itself for miles and miles to the east; while from the upper windows the western view embraces all that beautiful country between the valley of the Overpeck and the Orange Mountains. The air is exceedingly clear and salubrious, and has proved extremely beneficial to invalids and children of delicate constitutions. The hotel is supplied with water from a clear, cool, and delicious spring in the forest, a mile to the westward. The pleasant and various ways of access make it a most desirable summer resort, particularly for gentlemen doing business in the city. The drives are exceeding beautiful, and extend for miles along the Hudson, affording entrancing views of the noble river and charming villas along its banks. The house can accommodate about five hundred guests. The rooms are large, en suite, completely, richly, and tastefully furnished. The proprietor, Mr. D. S. Hammond, thoroughly understands his business, and nothing is left undone that could please the most exacting guest. The cuisine of the house is equal to any in the country. The grounds about the house are picturesque, the walks charming, and the river convenient for yachting and boating. Gas, hot and cold water, and new bath houses are provided, by which all the advantages of the salt water are made available. An excellent bill and-room and bowling-alley, a fine band of music, and a well-managed livery stable provide every comfort and recreation that could be expected. The fact that the first guests of the Mountain House continue to be its steadfast patrons, year after year, speaks for its special merits and healthfulness more plainly than many words. Among the attractions of Englewood, particularly for families, is the fine Collegiate Institute of the Rev. T. G. Wall, for young ladies and children, and the Englewood Classical and Mathematical School for boys.

PALISADES MOUNTAIN HOUSE, ENGLEWOOD, N. J.
On the Hudson River opposite Spuyten Duyvil.

ROSSMORE HOTEL, Broadway, 42d St., and Seventh Ave., New York, three blocks west of Grand Central Depot, CHARLES R. LELAND, Proprietor. Also Proprietor of the famous Delavan House of Albany and the celebrated Clarendon Hotel of Saratoga Springs, N. Y. Prices, $4.00 per day

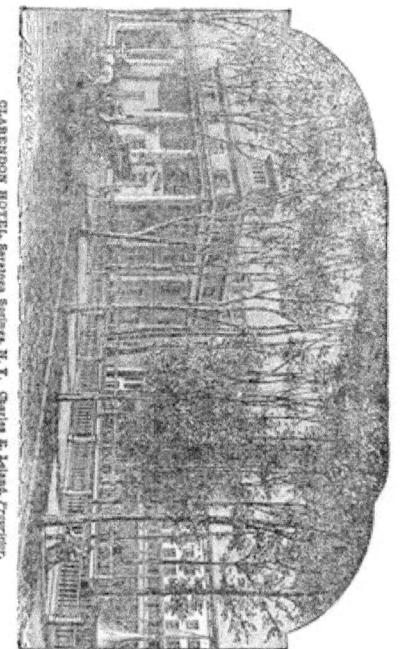

CLARENDON HOTEL, Saratoga Springs, N. Y. Charles E. Leland, Proprietor. Also Proprietor of the famous Delavan Hotel of Albany and the new and elegant Rossmore Hotel, Broadway, 41st Street and Seventh Avenue, New York City. Prices, $4.00 per day.

ARLINGTON HOTEL,

At WASHINGTON, D.C.

T. ROESSLE & SON, Proprietors.

The *Arlington Hotel* is well worthy of the first-class patronage which it receives. It is situated on the corner of 15th and H streets, in one of the most interesting portions of the city. The southern wing fronts the beautiful Lafayette Park, in which is the celebrated bronze equestrian statue of Jackson, and opposite which are the "White House," U. S. Treasury Building, and the U. S. War and Navy Departments. The residence of the Secretary of State is a few rods to the north of the hotel—and all the public buildings are within easy distance. The hotel is five stories high, with brown stone front, and is furnished in elegant style, and supplied with a fine passenger elevator—closets on all the floors, signal bells, etc. The dining hall is one of the handsomest and most pleasantly situated in Washington. A large number of the rooms are arranged in suites, with all the conveniences for family use. The proprietors of the Arlington, also conduct the magnificent *Fort William Henry Hotel at Lake George*, the finest summer resort in America. To the patrons of the *Fort William Henry* we need only say that what *it* is in the *summer resort* world the *Arlington* is among the hotels of the Capital.

FORT WILLIAM HENRY HOTEL.

T. ROESSLE & SON, Proprietors.   LAKE GEORGE, CALDWELL, N. Y.

"AMERICAN."

BOSTON.

The Largest First-Class Hotel

IN NEW ENGLAND.

Prices Reduced to $3, $3.50, and $4 per day, according to location of room.

CONVENIENTLY LOCATED FOR PLEASURE OR BUSINESS.

CONTAINS

PASSENGER ELEVATOR,

SUITS AND SINGLE APARTMENTS,

WITH

BATH ROOMS AND CLOSETS ADJOINING.

Noted throughout the country for its cleanliness and comfort.

BILLIARD HALLS, TELEGRAPH OFFICE AND CAFÉ.

LEWIS RICE & SON.

HAYNES'S HOTEL, Springfield, Mass.
POPULAR PRICES—1876; CHARGES ACCORDING TO ROOMS.
The largest first class house in the city. Special accommodations for families and large parties. Location unsurpassed. Six blocks down town from the Railroad Station; directly in the center of the city. Free from all noise, smoke and confusion of trains. Recently enlarged and greatly improved, making it the most complete Hotel Establishment in Western Massachusetts. The best rooms, best table, best service in the city. Post Office and Telegraph Office in the Rotunda. Porters, Baggage Wagons and Free Carriage to all trains.
THE MOST PERFECT PASSENGER ELEVATOR IN THE WORLD.

BRIGHT'S DISEASE,

Diabetes, Dropsy, Catarrh, Calculus, Gravel, Gout, Rheumatism, Dyspepsia,

DISEASES OF THE HEART, BLOOD, LIVER, KIDNEYS, BLADDER, PROSTATE GLAND, PREMATURE DEBILITY, CHRONIC AND FEMALE DISEASES HITHERTO INCURABLE. PAMPHLETS EXPLAINING THEIR SUCCESSFUL TREATMENT BY

ASAHEL, MADE OF GOD,
World Peerless Mineral Spring Water,
—AND—
DR. A. HAWLEY HEATH,
AUTHOR AND PROPRIETOR, FREE

Depot and Reception Rooms, No. 200 Broadway, New York.

Reduced to Twenty-Five Cents a Gallon per Barrel.

ALBANY AND NEW YORK
DAY LINE
ON THE HUDSON RIVER.

Summer Arrangement for Pleasure Travel.

THE STEAMBOATS
C. VIBBARD AND DANIEL DREW
LEAVE NEW YORK DAILY
(SUNDAYS EXCEPTED).

GOING NORTH.		GOING SOUTH.	
NEW YORK:	A.M.		A.M.
Vestry Street	8.10	*ALBANY*	8.30
W. 24th Street	8.30	*Hudson*	10.40
Nyack and Tarrytown, { By Ferryboat	9.55	*Catskill*	11.00
			P.M.
West Point	11.15	*Rhinebeck*	12.20
Newburgh	11.50	*Poughkeepsie*	1.15
	P.M.	*Newburgh*	2.10
Poughkeepsie	12.40	*West Point*	2.40
Rhinebeck	1.35	*Nyack and Tarrytown,* { By Ferryboat	4.05
Catskill	2.55	*NEW YORK:*	
Hudson	3.15	*W. 24th Street*	5.30
ALBANY	5.40	*Vestry Street*	5.50

CONNECTING AT ALBANY WITH ALL POINTS NORTH AND WEST.

☞ TRIP TICKETS from New York to West Point and Newburgh, returning same day, $1.00.

TICKETS or COUPONS good on Hudson River Railroad are received on board for passage.

MEALS CAN BE HAD ON THE BOATS.

Leave Albany at 8:30 A.M. on arrival of Chicago Express, on the New York Central Railroad.

ISAAC L. WELSH, G. T. A., New York.

DRS. STRONG'S REMEDIAL INSTITUTE,
SARATOGA SPRINGS, N. Y.,
Is open all the year, and is also a Summer Resort during the Visiting Season.

THE Institute has recently been doubled in size to meet the necessities of its increased patronage. It is now the largest health institution in Saratoga, and is unsurpassed in the variety of its remedial appliances by any in this country. In the elegance and completeness of its appointments it is unequaled. The building is heated by steam, so that in the coldest weather the air of the house is like that of midsummer. The proprietors, DRS. S. S. & S. E. STRONG, are Graduates of the Medical Department of the New York University, and are largely patronized by the medical profession. In addition to the ordinary remedial agencies used in general practice, they employ the EQUALIZER, or VACUUM TREATMENT, ELECTRO-THERMAL BATHS, SULPHUR AIR-BATHS, RUSSIAN BATHS, TURKISH BATHS, HYDROPATHY, MOVEMENT CURE, OXYGEN GAS, GYMNASTICS, HEALTH-LIFT, FARADAIC AND GALVANIC ELECTRICITY, LARYNGOSCOPE, &c., for the treatment of *Nervous, Lung, Female,* and *Chronic Diseases.* Its boarding department is of the highest order, and its society very superior.

REFERENCES.—Bishop M. Simpson, D.D., LL.D.; Rev. T. L. Cuyler, D.D.; Prof. Taylor Lewis, LL.D.; Chauncey N. Olds, LL.D.; Robert Carter, Esq.

☞ For particulars of the Institution, send for Circulars on Lung, Nervous, Female, and Chronic Diseases, and on our Appliances.

Address **DRS. S. S & S. E. STRONG**, Remedial Institute,
Saratoga Springs, N. Y.

PEOPLE'S LINE OF STEAMBOATS.

NEW YORK TO ALBANY

STEAMERS:

ST. JOHN,	DREW,
CAPT. T. D. CHRISTOPHER,	CAPT. S. J. ROE,
MONDAY,	TUESDAY,
WEDNESDAY,	THURSDAY,
FRIDAY.	SATURDAY.

From Pier 41, North River, South side of Canal Street, Near Jersey City Ferry, Desbrosses Street,

AT SIX O'CLOCK, P. M.

Connecting with trains of New York Central, Albany and Susquehanna, Rensselaer and Saratoga, and Boston and Albany Railroads.

Tickets can be had at the Office on the Wharf, to all points West and North— Adirondacks, White Mountains, via Lake George and L. Champlain, &c., &c. Also at Dodd's Express Office, 944 Broadway, and No. 4 Court Street, Brooklyn, and Baggage checked to destination. Telegraph Office on the Wharf.

Passengers leaving WASHINGTON at 8 A.M., BALTIMORE at 9:25 A.M., PHILADELPHIA at 1:30 P.M., arrive at NEW YORK at 5:15 P.M.—in time to connect as above.

MEALS ON THE EUROPEAN PLAN.

ALBANY TO NEW YORK.

STEAMERS:

DREW,	ST. JOHN,
CAPT. S. J. ROE,	CAPT. T. D. CHRISTOPHER,
MONDAY,	TUESDAY,
WEDNESDAY,	THURSDAY,
FRIDAY.	SATURDAY.

From STEAMBOAT LANDING, on arrival of trains of New York Central, Albany & Susquehanna, Rensselaer & Saratoga, and Boston & Albany Railroads. Arriving in New York in time to connect with trains South and East. Cars of Rens. & Sar. R. R. take passengers to Boats.

Tickets to Newark, New Brunswick, Trenton, Burlington, Philadelphia, Wilmington, Baltimore, and Washington City for sale on the Boats, and Baggage checked to destination.

For delivery of baggage, apply to Baggage Masters on Boats, Hudson River R.R. Tickets taken for passage, including State-Room Berth. Rooms heated by Steam during cool months.

JOHN C. HEWITT, G. T. Agent.

THE
CONGRESS AND EMPIRE
Spring Waters of Saratoga,

ARE THE BEST OF ALL THE SARATOGA WATERS FOR THE USE OF PERSONS OF CONSTIPATED HABIT.

They act promptly and pleasantly, without producing debility, and their effect is not weakened by continued use, as is the case with ordinary cathartics. At the same time they are not *too cathartic—a fault with some of our most drastic mineral waters*—but sufficiently so for daily and healthful use, and not strong enough to produce reaction.

Their continued use keeps the blood in a very pure and healthful condition, producing a clear florid complexion. They preserve the tone of the stomach, and are powerful preventives of fever and bilious complaints.

THE COLUMBIAN SPRING WATER

Is universally acknowledged to be the best *Chalybeate Water known*. Where the blood requires *iron*, this water supplies it in the best possible form for use. The assimilation is perfect. *A grain of iron in this water is*, in the opinion of a celebrated physician, "*more potent than twenty grains exhibited according to the Pharmacopœia.*"

These waters, being purely natural, are highly recommended, and very frequently prescribed by the best medical authorities, many of whom, however, have expressed their condemnation in strong terms of the use of *artificial* mineral waters.

Every genuine bottle of Congress Water has a large "**C**" raised on the glass.

FOR SALE BY DRUGGISTS and HOTELS THROUGHOUT the COUNTRY.

None Genuine Sold on Draught.

At our General Mineral Water Depot, in New York, all varieties of Natural Waters for sale at proprietors' prices, delivered and shipped to New York, Brooklyn, and Jersey City, *free of charge*.

Orders by mail will receive prompt attention. Empties taken back and allowed for at liberal prices. Address,

CONGRESS AND EMPIRE SPRING CO.,
94 Chambers Street, New York City,
Or, SARATOGA SPRINGS, N. Y.

☞ In connection with a recent analysis of Congress Water, Prof. Chandler says:

"As a *Cathartic* water, its almost entire freedom from iron should recommend it above all others, many of which contain so much of this ingredient as to seriously impair their usefulness."

FALL RIVER LINE

Between New York and Boston
VIA NEWPORT AND FALL RIVER.

STEAMERS LEAVE NEW YORK AT

5 P.M. Daily (Sundays, June 11th to Sept. 10th, inclusive,) from Pier 28, N. R., ft. of Murray St.; 4 P.M. in winter.

THE WORLD-RENOWNED STEAMERS

BRISTOL.	**PROVIDENCE.**
COMMANDER, A. G. SIMMONS.	COMMANDER, B. M. SIMMONS.

Trains leave Boston from the Old Colony R. R. Depot, corner South and Kneeland Sts., at 4:30 and 6 P. M., (and Sundays, June 11th to Sept. 10th, inclusive, at 7 P. M.,) connecting with these magnificent Steamers at Fall River.

Steamers leave Newport at 8:30 P. M.

The Very Best Route to and from New York, Boston, Taunton, New Bedford, Martha's Vineyard, Nantucket, Cape Cod, the White Mountains, and all points East, South, and West.

MUSIC.

The Management having in view the ENTERTAINMENT as well as the COMFORT AND SAFETY of their patrons, have at great expense engaged, for the season of pleasure travel, Hall's Celebrated Reed, String and Brass Bands, which will entertain passengers every evening with a *GRAND PROMENADE CONCERT.*

FOR TICKETS AND STATEROOMS

in New York, apply at 529 Broadway; Broadway, cor. 23d St.; Dodd's Express Office, 944 Broadway; and 4 Court St., Brooklyn, at all principal Hotels and Ticket Offices, at the Office on the Pier, and on board of Steamers.

In Boston, at No 3 Old State House and at Old Colony R. R. Depot.

Through Tickets sold by all the principal Railroads East, South and West. Baggage checked to destination.

THE ONLY DIRECT LINE TO AND FROM NEWPORT.

☞ Ask for Tickets via Fall River Line.

J. R. KENDRICK, Sup't,   BORDEN & LOVELL, Agents,
O. C. S. E., Boston.   O. C. S. B. Co., New York.

GEO. L. CONNOR, Gen'l Pass'r Agt. O. C. S. B. Co., New York.

THE "BRUNSWICK,"
Boylston Street, cor. of Clarendon, Boston, Mass.

A new strictly first-class Hotel. Conveniently located in the most fashionable part of the city. Fire-proof—all modern improvements.
J. W. WOLCOTT, Proprietor.

WESTMINSTER HOTEL,
Sixteenth Street and Irving Place, New York City.

Centrally located. Affords accommodations of peculiar excellence. European Plan. CHAS. B. FERRIN, Prop'r.

Best Religious Weekly Newspaper Published.

1826. ESTABLISHED FIFTY YEARS. **1876.**

THE CHRISTIAN ADVOCATE.

THE METROPOLITAN NEWSPAPER of the M. E. CHURCH.

C. H. FOWLER, D.D., LL.D., Editor.   W. H. DePUY, D.D., Assistant Editor.

The LEADING OFFICIAL CHURCH PAPER, whose name heads this page, is justly acknowledged to be the ablest and best religious weekly in the country, and now in its fiftieth year is still rapidly gaining in popularity, not alone in the families of the church whose interests it represents, but among the membership of sister denominations. Notwithstanding the great competition on every side, its patronage is increasing at home, and extends into every Christian country. It is not only the oldest and most widely circulated weekly Methodist journal in the world, but also has the largest subscription-list of any one of the great denominational weeklies.

(CIRCULATION 50,000 COPIES WEEKLY.)

A large number of leading banking, mercantile, manufacturing, and publishing houses in the principal cities have been steady patrons of its advertising columns, and recommend it highly as a first-class medium of communication between the better class of buyers and sellers, and prove their faith in it by their constant patronage.

A specimen copy of the Advocate, with the rates of advertising, will be sent free to any address on application to

NELSON & PHILLIPS, Publishers, 805 B'way, New York.

SARATOGA GEYSER SPRING.

THE CELEBRATED SPOUTING SPRING OF SARATOGA.

This wonderful mineral fountain was discovered in February, 1870. It is located on the Ballston avenue, one and a half miles south of principal hotels, at Saratoga Springs. The water vein was struck by the drill in the bird's-eye limestone one hundred and thirty-two feet beneath the surface rock. The orifice, bored in the rock, is five and a half inches in diameter, and 132 feet deep, and is tubed with a block-tin pipe, encased with iron, to the depth of eighty-five feet. Analysis of one U. S. Gallon by Professor C. F. Chandler, Ph.D., of Columbia College School of Mines:

Chloride of Sodium	502.080 grains.	Bicarbonate of Baryta	2.014 grains.
Chloride of Potassium	24.634 "	Bicarbonate of Iron	0.979 "
Bromide of Sodium	2.212 "	Sulphate of Potassa	0.313 "
Iodide of Sodium	0.248 "	Phosphate of Soda	trace.
Fluoride of Calcium	trace.	Biborate of Soda	trace.
Bicarbonate of Lithia	9.064 "	Alumina	trace.
Bicarbonate of Soda	71.332 "	Silica	0.005 "
Bicarb. of Magnesia	149.541 "	Organic matter	trace.
Bicarbonate of Lime	168.572 "		
Bicarbonate of Strontia	0.425 "	Total solid contents	931.546 "

Carbonic Acid Gas in 1 U. S. Gal .... 454.682 cub. in.
Density 1.011
Temperature .... 49° Fah.

It will be observed that the water is strongly charged with valuable medicinal, mineral and gaseous properties, and the preponderance of Gas enables the water to hold its heavy and valuable mineral elements in perfect solution, whereby the water is bottled in perfect purity, and may be preserved for ages and in any climate. The fact that the Spring is located 132 feet beneath a solid rock renders it free from all impurities from surface wash or drainage.

The water never varies in flavor, nor are its properties subjected to change by the dilution of fresh water or the mingling of foreign substances during the wet seasons of the year.

As a medicinal agency its effects are marvelous, especially in cutaneous diseases or any of the various phases of Scrofula, also in Kidney Disease, Liver Complaint, Dyspepsia, Biliousness, Rheumatism, Acidity of Stomach, Constipation, and Piles.

Geyser Water is a powerful cathartic, while at the same time, by proper use, its minerals may be retained to operate as a tonic and builder up of an enfeebled system. Geyser Water operates with excellent effect upon the Kidneys.

The latter found in it is a specific for gravel or stone, and is effectual in dissolving the chalk or limestone and uric deposits in Rheumatism and Gout.

As an Aperient or Cathartic the water should be taken in the morning.

It is sold in cases of four dozen Pints, two dozen Pints, or two dozen Quarts, and in Block Tin-Lined Barrels containing 30 gallons, for draught by druggists.

The Spring property is not managed by a Stock Company, and for the purposes of business the proprietor has adopted only the name "Geyser Spring."

Address GEYSER SPRING,
JACOB M. ADAMS, Prop'r. Saratoga Springs, N. Y.

United States Ink Man'fg Co.

BLACK WATER-PROOF WRITING INK.

Will not blur or spread when exposed to the action of water in any way, for any length of time. Is Black when first written with.

Is Absolutely Non-corrosive.

Does not gum up the pen.

Our Copying (and Writing) Fluid is superior to any in the market, foreign or domestic.

Superior Colored Inks and Mucilage.

Our Liquid Bluing is the purest and best in the market. Four times as economical as any other.

The SOUGHT AFTER HAIR RESTORER

is manufactured by Mr. L. Wilkins of the Company. Is the best article known for Restoring grey hair to its original color. Is not a dye. Does not injure the hair or head.

SALESROOMS, No. 49 DEY STREET,
NEW YORK CITY.

AWARDED THE HIGHEST MEDAL AT VIENNA.

E. & H. T. ANTHONY & CO.,
591 BROADWAY, NEW YORK,
(Opp. Metropolitan Hotel.)

Manufacturers, Importers and Dealers in

Chromos and Frames, Stereoscopes and Views,
ALBUMS, GRAPHOSCOPES, and SUITABLE VIEWS.

PHOTOGRAPHIC MATERIALS.

We are Headquarters for everything in the way of

STEREOPTICONS AND MAGIC LANTERNS,
Being Manufacturers of the

Micro-Scientific Lantern,	Stereo-Panopticon,
University Stereopticon,	Advertiser's Stereopticon,
Artopticon,	School Lantern,
Family Lantern,	People's Lantern.

Each style being the best of its class in the market. Catalogues of Lanterns and Slides, with directions for using, sent on application.

ANY ENTERPRISING MAN CAN MAKE MONEY WITH A MAGIC LANTERN.

Visitors to the Centennial are invited to examine our display at the Exposition in Photographic Hall, and to call on us at our Store in New York.

On your way to the Centennial, stop in New York and have your Photograph taken by **ABM. BOGARDUS**, the Art Photographer of thirty years' experience. Every man, woman and child should have some of my exquisite pictures to show how you looked in the Centennial Year of American Independence. Remember my Gallery is 872 Broadway, cor. of 18th Street, only. No connection with other Galleries carried on by persons pretending to be my successors. Block below and opposite Arnold, Constable & Co's.

"Fulfills the condition of a Family Sewing Machine far better than any other machine in the market."—*Judges' Report, American Institute Fair.*

NEW
WILLCOX & GIBBS
AUTOMATIC
SILENT SEWING MACHINE.

Awarded the grand "Gold Medal of Progress," of the American Institute, Nov., 1873, and the "Scott Legacy Medal," of the Franklin Institute, Oct., 1873.

No other Sewing Machine in the world has an "AUTOMATIC TENSION," or any other of its characteristic features.

WILLCOX & GIBBS S. M. Co.

invite the public to inspect this marvel of Sewing Machine mechanism—unquestionably the greatest invention in Sewing Machines since their introduction; completely revolutionizes the art of machine sewing. Visitors are delighted.

Call and examine, or send for full Descriptive Catalogue.

Perfect and durable Work always assured
No Instruction or Experience required.
No Ripping.
Most Powerful Feed ever invented.
The Only Machine in the World with Automatic Tension.
New Stitch Regulator.
Absolutely Noiseless in operation.
Other New and Valuable Features.

WILLCOX & GIBBS S. M. Co.,
658 BROADWAY,
COR. OF BOND STREET,   NEW YORK.

THE HEALTH-LIFT
Reduced to a Science.

CUMULATIVE EXERCISE.

A Thorough Gymnastic System
IN TEN MINUTES ONCE A DAY.

Health restored and Muscular Strength developed by equalizing and invigorating the circulation. The result of twenty years practical and theoretical study and experiment. The only scientific system of physical training. Minimum time for maximum results.

This "cut" represents a lady taking an exercise on the

Reactionary Lifter.

It will be seen that the EXERCISE, as well as the APPARATUS, is especially adapted for Ladies use. It is the only Machine in use by which a lady can take sufficient exercise without change of dress, soiled hands, awkward positions, etc. By its use, ten minutes once a day, they can get all needed exercise.

You are cordially invited to visit the

LADIES' PARLORS
OF THE

New York Health-Lift Company,
46 EAST FOURTEENTH STREET,
Bet Broadway and University Place, NEW YORK.

JOHN F. TROW & SON,
PRINTERS
AND
BOOKBINDERS,

Combine in their Extensive Premises,

205-213 EAST TWELFTH ST.
AND
15 VANDEWATER ST.,
NEW YORK,

The resources of the Old and Well-known Houses of JOHN F. TROW, ROBERT CRAIGHEAD, and C. A. ALVORD.

They are constantly adding improvements, both in the

BINDING AND PRINTING DEPARTMENTS,

And offer to Publishers facilities unequalled in this country for the
RAPID AND ACCURATE PRODUCTION OF BOOKS.

ALL ORDERS FOR
JOB PRINTING
Promptly attended to.

Estimates for Binding or Printing furnished on application.

SMITH'S PARLOR BED DEPOT.

Bookcase, SOFA, and Lounge Beds A Specialty.

Also, Ladies' Cutting Table and Folding Chairs.
816 Broadway, Near 12th Street, **NEW YORK**

PORTABILITY

combined with great power in FIELD, MARINE, TOURISTS', OPERA, and general out-door day and night double perspective glasses; will show objects distinctly from twice six miles. Spectacles of the greatest transparent power, to strengthen and improve the sight without the distressing result of frequent changes. Catalogues sent by inclosing stamp.
SEMMONS, Occulists' Optician, 687 Broadway, N. Y.

COLLEGE SONGS.

CARMINA YALENSIA:

A New Collection of Yale and other College Songs, with Music and Piano-Forte Accompaniments, and Engraving of Yale College Buildings. Extra cloth, $1.75. Extra cloth, full gilt, $2.25.

CARMINA COLUMBIANA:

A New Collection of Columbia College Songs, with Music and Piano-Forte Accompaniments. Bound in extra cloth, showing the Columbia College colors, blue and white. Price, $1.75.

HAPPY HOURS: a New Song-Book for Schools, Academies, and the Home Circle. 188 pp. 12mo. Price, board covers, 50 cents. Cloth, 75 cents.

Any of above books sent by mail, post-paid, on receipt of price.

TAINTOR BROTHERS & CO., PUBLISHERS,
758 Broadway, New York

Life Insurance an Element of Success.

THE successful man makes the most of every advantage which nature and circumstance have placed within his reach. He carefully considers his mental abilities and inclinations, and pursues that course for which reason tells him that he is best fitted. The circumstances of his birth and education as well as his physical condition and bodily powers go to influence his pursuits. Every circumstance is then embraced to further his plans. His mind is called upon to assist him to the extent of its forces, and his body should likewise contribute its share to the general fund.

The man who is so fortunate as to possess a sound mind in a sound body, and who desires to make the most of both, cannot consistently neglect the advantages which Life Insurance offers to him. His neighbor may have the elements of success in an equal degree, but some weakness, perhaps unnoticed before, debars him from Life Insurance. The gift of health should thus form an important element in the working capital of him who possesses it, and the taking advantage of the superiority which its possession for the time being gives may be the turning point of success. A Life Policy taken in health and prosperity may be just the security needed in financial troubles, and certainly will be when health is gone and Life Insurance can no longer be obtained.

In choosing a company, that one should be selected which is most careful in the selection of its members, that good health may receive the greatest possible benefits. *The Phœnix Mutual Life Insurance Company of Hartford, Conn.,* issues policies on none but the best of risks. It has had 25 years of successful experience, and has assets of the most unquestionable character, of over $10,000,000, invested for the security of its policy-holders. Its business is conducted with economy and prudence, and its members receive the benefits arising from a conservative management to their fullest extent.

AARON C. GOODMAN, *President.*

JONATHAN B. BUNCE, *Vice-Pres.* JOHN M. HOLCOMBE, *Sec'y.*

POND'S EXTRACT
OF
HAMAMELIS, OR WITCH HAZEL,
The People's Remedy,

For Piles, Sprains, Lameness, Burns, Scalds, Bruises, Soreness, Rheumatism, Boils, Ulcers, Catarrh, Wounds, etc. Also for Toothache, Headache, Neuralgia, Sore Throat, Hoarseness, Colic, Diarrhœa, and all Hemorrhages, &c.

RETAIL PRICES.—Small......$0.50—cheap, because doses are small.
Medium....$1.00—worth $1.38; saving 38 cents.
Large......$1.75—worth $2.67; saving 92 cents.

This popular remedy has now been before the country for more than a quarter of a century, during which, with very little advertising, it has firmly established itself in the confidence of the people; and in thousands of families has become as indispensable as flour or salt.

During this period its inherent merits have overcome the intense prejudice of physicians, and it is now daily prescribed and recommended by members of the Faculty, of all Schools—Allopathic, Homœopathic, Botanic, and Eclectic. Ask any of them about it. They will tell you that the medicinal virtues of WITCH HAZEL is an extraordinary range of action are indisputable, and that ours is simply the

BEST AND ONLY UNIFORM PREPARATION

from that shrub; that it is carefully made by experienced pharmacists, having the advantage of the perfect machinery required by an enormous business, from the best parts of the plant, judiciously selected at an exact and critical period of its growth. They will tell you that it is *always the same, and always good*; that it is not affected by change of climate or temperature; that its action is prompt and effectual; that it does not accumulate in the system, and ultimately manifest poisonous characteristics, but may be used freely, externally and internally, alone or in connection with other medicines,

WITHOUT THE SLIGHTEST DANGER.

Ask your druggist for one of the little books (bearing his address), with which we supply him free, for distribution among his patrons. If you are well, it may give you some *Interesting and Useful Information;* while to the ill it may be the *Road to Health.*

REMEMBER.—POND'S EXTRACT really has a very extensive range of action. It will promptly relieve any pain, and will effectually and permanently cure a greater number of the ills which an intelligent and prudent mother would trust herself to treat than any other preparation. It is, therefore,

AN INVALUABLE DOMESTIC REMEDY.

The 50c. Bottle is cheap, because the doses are small. The $1 Bottle is cheaper, worth $1.38, saving 38c. The $1.75 Bottle is cheapest, worth $2.67, saving 92c.

FOR SALE EVERYWHERE.

POND'S EXTRACT

Charter Oak Life Insurance Company,
HARTFORD, CONN.

ASSETS,
$14,500,000.

ANNUAL INCOME,
$4,000,000.

Life Insurance Policies issued on all the usual plans at lowest Money Rates.

Policies on the DEPOSIT PLAN, for terms of ten or fifteen years, with peculiar advantages in case of discontinuance, are highly recommended. Send for circulars describing the plan in detail.

E. R. WIGGIN, President.

S. H. WHITE, Vice-Pres. and Treas. A. H. DILLON, Jr., 2d Vice-Pres.
HARRY STEVENS, Secretary. WM. L. SQUIRE, Ass't Secretary.
H. J. FURBER, Financial Manager.

R. O. GODWIN, General Agent, 161 Broadway, New York.
Geo. B. Hilliard, 158 Washington St., Boston.
Wylie & Mann, 1 Tribune Building, Chicago.

THE LEADING CLOTHIERS.

Our two Stores are constantly supplied with the best Stock of Clothing in New York.

We state the material plainly on each Garment.

We sell at one price.

We guarantee entire satisfaction.

We give special attention to Custom orders.

DEVLIN & CO.,
Broadway, cor. Grand St., Broadway, cor. Warren St.,
NEW YORK.

www.ingramcontent.com/pod-product-compliance
Lightning Source LLC
Chambersburg PA
CBHW031455160426
43195CB00010BB/986